THE FIRST HUNDRED DAYS

How to Hit the Ground Running
With a Brand-New Job

Jeffrey Tarter

D1166265

For

JANE
FIRST READER
Who always believes I can do better,
and is ~~often right~~*

*CORRECTION: *"usually right"... jane*

Cover illustration by Simon Streatfeild, Nomis Animation
Back cover photo by Jonathan Sachs

Kindle edition:
ISBN-978-0-9970303-0-3

Print edition:
ISBN-13: 978-1519234438
ISBN-10: 1519234430

Contents

CHAPTER 1
The First Hundred Days

"Now, Voyager, sail thou forth, to seek and find."
— Walt Whitman

The moment you show up for Day One of your new job, the rules of the career game change dramatically. That well-crafted resume that helped you get a foot in the door? Irrelevant. Those shrewd answers you gave during your interviews? Forgotten. Your test scores, internships, awards, references? Buried in a filing cabinet in the HR department.

Instead, you now find yourself meeting bunches of people whose names and titles you struggle to remember. They're busy doing… well, stuff. You probably have a guide who shows you your new desk, phone, computer, office supplies, and a fat employee handbook that describes official holidays and the dental plan. Is this really your reward for a long, hard job search? Will there be a quiz?

If you're starting your first "real" job (that is, a job that could make a big difference to your career path), this launchpad experience is likely to be intimidating. That's not because employers want to test your courage — in fact, just the opposite. Your new company has invested a fair amount of effort and cash to find *you* and convince you to come aboard. If you fail, that investment goes down the drain.

Your new employers also understand — or they should — that you're walking into a confusing new world. They know that even a small company is an extraordinarily complicated machine. It takes a while for anyone, rookie or veteran, to figure out the informal rules that govern each company's inner workings, as well as the personal histories, the spider web of relationships, and the occasional briar patches that entangle the unwary. If you ask for a little help, your new colleagues won't think you're a loser.

But — you'll get off to a faster start if you're at least somewhat prepared. That's the reason for this book: to identify field-tested techniques for success during your "first hundred days" on a new job and to offer insights into what is often a life-changing experience. We've drawn on the experience of hundreds of employees, managers, advisors, and experts in a wide spectrum of organizations, and we've tried to distill their knowledge into actionable advice. You'll probably already know *some* of the suggestions they share—but it's safe to say that even the best-prepared rookie can always benefit from extra advice and coaching. That's how you win the game.

Of course, you already know that there's no single paint-by-numbers formula for succeeding in a new job. There are no standard-issue employees, no cookie-cutter companies, no universal job descriptions. But there's also a lot of common ground to most new-job experiences. If you understand the various rules for success that are widely shared, you'll probably have a much easier time mastering the unusual cases.

Welcome!

Why a Hundred Days?

Millions of words have been written about how to achieve career success. Much of this advice is wonderful and wise… but it often comes too late to do much good. If you've spent the last five years building your reputation as a mediocre employee, let's be honest: If a genie magically transformed you into a star performer, would the people around you even notice? Or believe their eyes? Probably not.

For better or worse, your single best chance to establish yourself as a rising star is when you start a new job. On Day One you start with a clean slate—no track record of performance, no relationships, no reputation. You may also have almost no authority over other people and no political leverage, but you'll never have more control over the direction of your own career. This is an opportunity to seize quickly.

A "new job" doesn't necessarily mean "your first job," incidentally. We live in a time of enormous job mobility, when lifetime employment in the same company and even the same job is considered a trifle eccentric. Every time you jump to a new company or take on a distinctly new assignment, you'll have a chance to re-launch your career. In fact, some of the world's best CEOs — people with decades of experience — screwed up a few times before a new job gave them another turn at bat.

But why a hundred days?

A hundred days has become a convenient milestone for fast-moving, high-impact campaigns. Napoleon swept back into power during a dramatic 100-day period after he escaped from exile in 1815; newly-elected Franklin Roosevelt rolled out most of his New Deal legislation during his first hundred days in office. Wall Street analysts use roughly the same period of time — three-month calendar quarters — to measure progress toward major financial and sales goals. As one journalist once said, "It's not a perfect measure, but it's a useful one."

In short, a hundred days is traditionally a chunk of time for measuring success at large-scale efforts. It's a realistic period for building momentum, for solving big problems (or big pieces of problems). It's enough time to demonstrate how good you are.

A less-obvious point about the hundred-day time period is that it creates a deadline, and deadlines do wonders for imparting a sense of urgency. If you take the advice in this book seriously (and we hope you do), you'll quickly realize you have a lot to accomplish — and that's not even including the day-to-day work that's part of your regular job description. You're going to be tempted to push the hard tasks into the future, and to slip into a comfortable rut. Almost everyone feels this temptation early in their careers.

But then one day you look at your life and find that getting out of that comfortable rut is really, really hard. "Oops. Where did I go wrong?"

You should also be aware that some employers now move very quickly when they feel they've made a hiring mistake. Recent U.S. Bureau of Labor Statistics data shows that new companies terminate roughly a quarter of their new hires within the first year. In a similar vein, a Wall Street Journal report found that "startup managers say they try to let underperformers or poor fits go within their first three months, but some hires don't last even that long." (Mature companies tend to be slower to pull the trigger on their hiring mistakes, but they're also known for layoffs that can impact literally thousands of employees at the same time.) You may have landed a great job, but there's no guarantee that you'll keep that job.

That's why we frame most of our advice in terms of a hundred-day deadline: To remind you that the clock is always running on your progress toward success. And if you don't achieve your whole agenda by the time you reach Day 100, just keep plugging away at whatever is left. You'll never really run out of ways to become a star.

A Few Questions

"Should I read this book?"

"Gosh, yes!" says our marketing consultant. "Every page is full of great advice! Stories! Checklists! Buy copies for your friends, too! You'll all live long and prosper!"

Well, okay. More to the point, there are three kinds of reader who will benefit from reading *The First Hundred Days:*

> **Newcomers to the job market,** especially recent grads with limited experience in the working world. You're our primary audience, in case that's not totally obvious.

> **Experienced employees** who are starting a new job after a first- or second-time work experience that didn't work out as well as you hoped.

> **Newly promoted employees** who are taking on new, unfamiliar responsibilities as managers and team leaders.

This is also a useful book for job-seekers who'd like a sneak peek at what lies ahead once they find a willing employer. And for parents whose offspring are still living at home, we offer advice that just might improve the chances that your dear ones will not just land a job but will also *keep* that job.

"Is this just a book about white-collar office jobs?"

Nope. Pretty much everything we talk about in the following pages applies to anyone who works with other people (bosses, teams, customers, and other employees), who produces some type of useful results, and who expects to make a positive impression on new work colleagues. If you happen to start your new career in retail, construction, medical, government, media, the arts, or education—you'll naturally need job-specific skills and talents. But you'll also need to master basic workplace and relationship skills that are remarkably similar across all industries and types of organizations. These workplace skills are the focus of this book.

"Is this a good book for entrepreneurs?"

Our emphasis in the following pages is on creating successful *personal careers*, not successful startups. Unlike books that offer advice to managers and entrepreneurs, *The First Hundred Days* addresses people who have very limited authority over their jobs, their company's products, and their working environment. We suspect that our readers will learn enough here to become far better entrepreneurs and executives when they move up the career ladder. But that's a few years down the road.

"What about cultural differences?"

The First Hundred Days is a guide for new job holders who work for U.S. companies (which tend to be the most demanding and productive in the world). We know that companies do many things differently in London, Paris, Hong Kong, and Mumbai—but that's another book. (And we'll leave that book to an author who understands what goes on during a three-day cricket match.)

However, if you happen to come from a different culture, *The First Hundred Days* will definitely help you better understand the U.S. working world—and even how to master our sometimes quirky rules for becoming a rising star.

"What if I don't want a high-stress, fast-track career?"

Then you won't become a Fortune 500 chief executive (sorry, if that's your dream). But job success is always relative. The recommendations you'll find in *The First Hundred Days* aren't just for would-be super-stars: They'll also help you become *relatively* more successful, more respected by your co-workers, and perhaps more secure when layoffs occur. You'll also get better assignments, a better shot at merit raises, and (hopefully) a healthier balance between your work and personal life. As you'll discover in Chapter 11, job satisfaction is one of the key factors we emphasize as part of your overall success.

In short, there's nothing wrong with being a competent, middle-of-the-road worker bee if that's your career goal. In fact, for many people that's the definition of career success. And *The First Hundred Days* can probably help you achieve that goal faster and perhaps with fewer false steps than you might have taken on your own.

CHAPTERS 2-4

Relationships

In the first few months on your new job, the personal relationships you develop are going to feel *different*. Different from how families interact, different from the classrooms you've occupied for many years, different from your circles of friends, probably even different from your experience with a small family business.

Most important, you'll find yourself in a much more complicated and structured world. You'll have well-defined responsibilities. Most of the people you'll work with will have authority—lots of authority—over your daily life. You'll be expected to work as part of a team with other people, and you'll find that working on a classroom project with a friend or discussing politics with your favorite aunt at Thanksgiving didn't prepare you for serious collaboration and knowledge sharing. And if your new company is struggling with internal political wars... well, hang on tight.

The following three chapters offer guidelines about how to develop these new relationships. If you build a strong foundation with your new boss, your new team, and your new networks, then you'll definitely be off to a good start.

CHAPTER 2

Relationships: Your Boss

"By working faithfully eight hours a day you
may eventually get to be boss and work twelve hours a day."
— Robert Frost

You probably met your boss while you were interviewing for your new job. You had an extended conversation about your expectations (and his or hers) and your boss listened closely when you described your strengths and weaknesses. Almost certainly, you and your boss aren't total strangers to each other.

In fact, there's a good chance you were hired *because* you made a positive impression on your new boss. Don't blow it now.

Over the next hundred days, how you interact with your new boss is likely to be the single most important day-to-day relationship in your budding career. Your new boss can be a source of advice and feedback on your performance, an influential advocate, and a primary decision-maker about the assignments that will help you show off your star potential.

But before this magic happens, you should recognize that there are two kinds of bosses: **hands-on** and **hands-off**. How well you get along with your new boss will depend greatly on whether you interact appropriately:

> **Hands-on bosses** are primarily people managers. Their top responsibility in the company is to work with team members, enhancing overall performance and output of the group they manage. When the team generates what seem to be weak results, hands-on bosses often believe the best solution is to jump in and micro-manage everyone. Hands-on bosses like teamwork, staff meetings, and frequent status reports.

> **Hands-off bosses** may manage a few employees, but their primary role involves working with clients or directly providing professional expertise (finance, law, creative services, medical care, etc.). Hands-off bosses tend to give

14

their team members a good deal of autonomy, but getting the full attention of a hands-off boss can be frustrating. In some organizations — schools, for example — a nominal boss may relinquish so much authority to senior staff members that employees come to feel that they don't even *have* a boss. In cases like this, it's usually wise to treat the boss's stand-ins as if they're running the show.

Of course, you'll need to discuss your boss's specific expectations and management preferences during your first post-hiring conversation... and you should follow up by talking with other team members who also report to your new boss. The success of your new relationship will depend heavily on how well you engage with the boss's personal management style.

If you haven't had much experience working with a boss, you may be astonished by the diversity of management styles you'll encounter even within a small company. One of the most important (and subtle) differences in style is how your boss *processes new information.* Management guru Peter Drucker argues that bosses are usually either "listeners" or "readers," and he says they often ignore information that reaches them through the wrong channels. This kind of communication failure can be disastrous, says Drucker:

> Lyndon Johnson destroyed his presidency, in large measure, by not knowing that he was a listener. His predecessor, John Kennedy, was a reader who had assembled a brilliant group of writers as his assistants, making sure that they wrote to him before discussing their memos in person. Johnson kept these people on his staff — and they kept on writing. He never, apparently, understood one word of what they wrote. Yet as a senator, Johnson had been superb; for parliamentarians have to be, above all, listeners.

Pay close attention to how your new boss handles meetings, decision-making, disagreements, stress, and missed goals. Since you're the junior member of this boss-employee relationship, it's largely up to you to make pragmatic adjustments to your own working style — do whatever works best, as well as you can. (As you build trust and personal authority, you can probably push back a bit. But not in your first hundred days.)

Regardless of your boss's specific management style, however, there are some basic guidelines that will get your relationship off to a good start:

✓ **First, never waste your boss's time:** Figure out the simple stuff on your own—how to find the supply cabinet or fill out an expense form. Use your face time with the boss to ask intelligent questions about project requirements, deadlines, resources, quality expectations, and workflow for your assignments. Plan your agenda carefully: You should never need to send a follow-up e-mail that says, "I forgot to ask you…"

✓ **Bring alternate solutions instead of problems:** Here's the kind of question bosses hate: "One of our bidders on the outsourcing contract just dropped out—what should I do next?" Bosses would much rather hear this: "Should I recruit a third bidder, or are we okay with just two bids?" Get into the habit of figuring out a Plan B for everything you do (and perhaps a Plan C, D, and E for important issues). When problems pop up—and they always do—your boss will begin to notice that you're usually well prepared.

✓ **Make sure your boss knows everything that matters:** This is tougher than it sounds. Bosses are swamped with lengthy reports and raw data dumps, which typically contain little relevant, actionable information. Rather than add to this problem, identify *key points* that might require the boss's action or a decision (a good rule of thumb is to present no more than two or three major points per report). Show trends and context (did customer satisfaction drop right after the new product hit the market, or do our scores always drop during the summer?). And never hide bad news—in fact, make a point of being direct and honest when there's a problem. Many bosses ignore all the happy talk they hear and dig until they find a single obscure failing (one cranky customer, a 5% budget overrun for February) and then go nuts. This is called "management by exception" and it will make your life miserable if your boss thinks you don't disclose the whole picture.

✓ **Meticulously organize your own work:** If your boss drops into your office to ask about the Acme Explosives contract, you should never say, "I think it's in my inbox. Or maybe in that stack over there..." Set up your files and records so you (or anyone else) can instantly retrieve active information. Record passwords, account numbers, contact names, software licenses, and other data. Document all your office procedures. Display project milestones on a bulletin board. Keep an appointment calendar that shows the status of every phone call and e-mail contact you're responsible for tracking. And so forth. If you vanished tomorrow, your replacement should be able to step in immediately.

✓ **Pick your time carefully:** If your boss is concentrating on a major client presentation or complex budget projections, even a brief interruption can bust up his concentration. Try to schedule your urgent problems so they can be handled at routine project meetings. And if your boss has a poster on the wall that says "Your lack of planning is not my emergency" — well, you've been warned.

✓ **Listen carefully to your boss's advice:** According to a large-scale survey by Leadership IQ, a coaching service, the single biggest reason why new hires fail is that "they can't accept feedback." The study found that 26% of failures (defined as people who were "terminated, left under pressure, received disciplinary action or significantly negative performance reviews") ignored advice from their bosses, colleagues, clients, and others. By comparison, only 11% failed because they lacked necessary technical skills. Your boss may be a jackass, but at least *try* to take his or her advice graciously. Ignoring feedback brands you as negative and argumentative, and that's almost always a big deal on your performance record.

★

The First Conversation

It's pretty standard practice for bosses to take new employees out to lunch (or make some comparable social gesture) to welcome them to the team and answer questions. Often, this conversation is just a formality: The new employee insists "everything is super, no questions, I'm glad to be aboard."

That's a bad way to get started. Your first extended conversation with your boss is an opportunity that may never get repeated. From now on, you and your boss will rarely talk about long-term expectations, your career, and other topics that aren't immediately work-related. So be prepared with at least three or four issues that only your boss can address:

✓ **What's the highest priority for the team in terms of results?** If your new boss says "Everything is a top priority," probe for details. Who are the department's most valued customers? Are deadlines more or less important than budgets? What metrics get the most attention from top management?

✓ **How can I ace my first annual assessment?** Be clear that you're determined to become a top team member, so you want to understand how your boss measures performance. One reason why employees hate the assessment process is random, undocumented criteria for rating employees. By raising the issue up front, you're giving your boss an opening to define a more objective approach.

✓ **Do you see any areas where I could use more experience or training?** Here's where you get insight into your immediate career path within the company. Again, probe for details if you can. How would you get "more experience"? Can your boss recommend training or classes? How about tutorials on the company's own products?

✓ **What's the department's biggest obstacle?** This question gives your boss a chance to open up and discuss personal frustrations, so be sure you've established some degree of trust before you ask it. If your boss has been evasive about earlier questions, move on.

Note that there is one question you should never raise during this first conversation: *How and when do I get a raise?* Wrong time, wrong place.

★

Surviving a Bad Boss

If you're lucky, you'll get a boss who's a wonderful character, likely to become a life-long friend. Great bosses are visionary leaders, their endorsements are influential throughout their industry, and they always find time to send thank-you notes when you've done a great job.

More likely, your new boss will be more or less adequate at his or her job and will be aware that taking care of you and the rest of the team is a responsibility that somehow has to fit into an already-crowded calendar.

And then there's the boss who's an incompetent jerk. Not just a hard task-master, but someone who sucks the air out of a room and makes you hate your job.

Sadly, a good many companies seem to have a high tolerance level for bad bosses, and their negative influence is remarkably destructive. According to an Inc. Magazine survey, "three out of every four employees report that their boss is the worst and most stressful part of their job and 65% of employees said they would take a new boss over a pay raise." Bad bosses are said to derail innovation, annoy customers, play favorites, hog the limelight, drive away top talent, and create perpetual uncertainty among their employees. One management consulting firm even found that bad bosses help break up marriages and ruin weekends (anxious employees spend an average of 6.2 hours every weekend worrying about their bosses, the consulting firm found).

What's behind this proliferation of bad bosses? Executive coach Bruce Tulgan claims that the core problem that many bosses face these days is simply finding enough hours in the day to do their job well. Bosses typically face relentless demands on their time, both from their own bosses and from the staff they're supposed to supervise, says Tulgan. They're perpetually stressed out.

One consequence of this time pressure, Tulgan adds, is "a shocking and profound epidemic of undermanagement":

> The vast majority of supervisory relationships between employees and their bosses lack the day-to-day engagement necessary to consistently maintain the very basics of management: clear expectations, necessary resources, real performance tracking, and fair credit and reward.

Ouch. That's a pretty grim description of what's supposed to be your most important working relationship.

In *It's Okay to Manage Your Boss,* Tulgan goes on to argue that most of the management behaviors that drive employees nuts — micromanagement, confusing instructions, procrastination, lack of respect for top performers — are symptoms of this "undermanagement." And undermanagement itself is what happens when bosses are too busy to hold up their end of a work relationship.

One solution that veteran employees use with stressed-out bosses is to cut them out of most decision-making. Just forge ahead, do what seems to be the right thing, and hope for the best. As the legendary Admiral Grace Hopper once said, "If it's a good idea, go ahead and do it. It is much easier to apologize than it is to get permission."

But for a newcomer, this is clearly a high-risk strategy. Better to keep your head down and hope that someone in your boss's chain of command is listening to the rumors. (Senior managers usually have a private intelligence network that keeps them aware of the worst jerks. Your new boss may already be on the way out.) Build a solid record of accomplishments and make friends in other parts of the company who can recommend you for openings in their departments.

At the same time, bear in mind that not all tyrannical bosses are genuine jerks. You may end up with a boss who's as green as you are—newly-promoted to a managerial job and overwhelmed by new responsibilities. If that seems to be the problem, giving your boss extra *personal* support may dramatically change the jerk-like behavior. It's worth a try.

In addition, many highly competitive industries—including Hollywood, the Internet, the media, and high fashion—often put new employees through a rugged "boot camp" entry-level period. The purpose is to weed out people who don't have enough passion about their careers for long-term success. If you think that's the reason your badly-behaved boss gives you a hard time, then (assuming you really want to succeed in this world) treat this experience as a test of your grit and determination.

★

The Loyalty Challenge

"I get along pretty well with my current boss, but my goal is to get promoted to a job in a different department," a reader asks. "I'm worried that my boss won't recommend me if I become too valuable to him."

This is a fair question. No boss really expects to hang on to a talented employee forever... but at the same time, the cost and hassle of replacing you is not going to be trivial. Career guru Donald Asher points out that an in-house promotion "creates two staffing changes; hiring from the outside involves only one." If you have scarce skills, if you're involved in a "critical, high-value project," if you've developed relationships with important clients—your boss will probably hang on to you like Super Glue.

Moreover, it's likely that you'll need your boss's *enthusiastic* endorsement for a promotion elsewhere in the company. In an insightful guide to upward mobility called *Who Gets Promoted,*

Asher makes the point that companies are sometimes wary about hiring internal candidates who seem a bit too outstanding:

> Top performers are by definition not like the rest of us. Many are difficult and temperamental people. They've lived in a world designed for the averages; they are often frustrated, or they may be rule-breakers. Are you known as reliable? Or are you a strong contributor with a tragic flaw, like a hot temper or a habit of blowing off assignments that don't interest you? When managers do risk analysis, they must project worst-case scenarios. If the risk is too great, all the benefits in the world will be passed over in favor of a less risky alternative.

So how do you escape the clutches of a boss who thinks you're terrific? Asher has some helpful thoughts:

On being easy to replace: "Irreplaceable people are *never* promoted," Asher warns. "In every organization there are some people who withhold critical data from others, refuse to delegate anything but the most mundane tasks, and retain all decision-making authority. Their absence from work, for even a day, brings their unit or department to a halt."

On training and cross-training your staff: "Teaching, training, developing, guiding, and mentoring your subordinates can be career-advancing practices," Asher says. Pay special attention to training your own replacement in case you do get promoted, he adds. "If you've done a good job of developing a subordinate, you may get the nod even if your rival for the promotion is a much better performer."

On developing an internal resume: Maintain a secret "brag sheet" of your current accomplishments that are tied to "an overarching organization goal or strategy." Constantly update this internal resume with your latest accomplishments, Asher adds. "If you hear about a great opportunity in a related department, you can drop your internal resume on that decision-maker and prevent him from posting the position, or you may become the frontrunner and keep him from seriously considering others."

On following the rules: "Rules govern internal job-seeking at most organizations. Some of these rules may be official, codified policies, while others are just prudent practice." One prudent practice, Asher adds, is always to notify your current boss when you're applying for an internal job. "No gossip travels faster than a story about someone applying for a new job."

Too Many Bosses

"I've started a new job in a small firm that's run by a husband and wife. The husband is the CEO, and his wife is general manager. Both keep giving me orders that contradict each other, and I'm about ready to quit. Is there any way to fix this awful situation?"

How hard have you tried to solve this problem? New employees can be surprisingly timid about confronting their bosses about relationship issues. You don't need to throw a temper tantrum, but your first step ought to be a polite, low-key discussion about your new company's chain of command. Avoid saying things like "awful situation" and "ready to quit" at this point—that's not going to solve the problem (you know that, right?). Instead, stick to the facts: "Last week, Helen asked me to reorganize all our client files by date, and then George said to put everything back into alphabetical order. And sometimes I'm covering the phones at lunch for Helen and then George sends me to the deli for sandwiches. I'm trying to do a good job here, but it's hard when I get conflicting instructions."

By describing actual incidents rather than generalities, you may make an astonishing discovery: The root cause of your problem is that you're too timid about talking with your boss (or bosses). Unless Helen and George are incredibly stupid, they're likely to acknowledge the problem and try to solve it with minimal confrontation. George may say, "You work for Helen—that's official. If I ask for a favor or make a suggestion, clear it with her if there's any conflict. Okay?" The rest is up to you.

Now, sometimes an employee ends up working for multiple bosses and the problem isn't just poor communication. Many firms have adopted a "shared resources" approach—employees with specialized skills are expected to work for whichever departments happen to need their services. These "shared" employees usually report to an administrative boss for assignments and scheduling, but their day-to-day work is supervised by other department managers or partners. Bigger companies call this arrangement "matrix management," and the jury is still out on whether it creates more efficiency than chaos.

The problem with matrix management, not surprisingly, is that multiple bosses tend to have multiple agendas. A programmer who's a "shared resource" on a big project may get orders to finish the job by the posted deadline no matter what gets in the way; meanwhile, the boss in charge of testing insists on rigorous quality assurance no matter what happens to the deadline. It's the Helen and George show all over again...

And sometimes the situation gets worse. Unlike Helen and George, your individual "matrix" bosses typically don't have much stake in you as an employee. You're expendable, like a shared printer. Stress and long hours are just part of your job description. And your nominal boss — a project manager, an IT team leader, a resource coordinator — almost certainly has little authority to resolve conflicts.

Some advice for surviving matrix management:

✓ **Keep a close eye on the schedule:** A project that's running a week late in August doesn't look like a crisis. But if there's a hard deadline at the end of December, somebody will have to work like crazy at year-end to make up the lost week. And forget about Christmas with your family. You and Santa Claus are both going to have a busy night.

✓ **If you spot a potential problem, alert your admin boss:** At least you'll be on the record — and your admin boss now has to find a manager with the authority to resolve the issue.

✓ **Find out who signs the check:** Divided authority often means that you'll run in circles trying to get a decision about spending money. Make sure it's clear from the beginning who's in charge of project budgets and who approves change orders.

✓ **Find out which boss controls your performance review:** Multiple bosses can mean multiple badly-informed perspectives on your value as an employee. The reward for your long hours and burnout may be that your great results become almost invisible.

CHAPTER 3

Relationships: Your Team

"Talent wins games, but teamwork wins championships."
— Michael Jordan

With the exception of one-person businesses, virtually all companies are essentially *team efforts*. The whole company team may consist of several million employees (Walmart, say, or McDonald's) or just a few family members (a mail-order website, a building contractor whose spouse keeps the books). But regardless of company size, the ability to work as a team is almost always an essential success factor.

In fact, teams exist for exactly the same reason your own job exists: *to produce results* (see Chapter 5). The difference is that teams typically produce bigger and better results than single employees can by working alone. If you've studied classical economics, you may remember Adam Smith's example of an 18th Century Scottish pin factory: Working alone, said Smith, a talented artisan could make "perhaps not one pin in a day." But a team of ten pin-makers working in a small factory, each specializing in a few tasks, "could make among them upwards of forty-eight thousand pins in a day. Each person, therefore, making a tenth part of forty-eight thousand pins, might be considered as making four thousand eight hundred pins in a day."

Since Adam Smith's day, we've learned that team efforts can have a similar multiplier effect on virtually every aspect of business activity, from the executive teams at the top of the organization to the hundreds of support departments, sales teams, and project groups that handle day-to-day operations. We honor the occasional superstar who delivers great results, but surprisingly often the superstar's core talent is an ability to leverage the performance of a team.

Especially in bigger companies, this proliferation of teams is often bewildering to people who have spent their lives in classrooms or small business settings, where teams tend to be less formal. "I didn't understand the difference between a 'boss' and a teacher," one new-minted graduate admitted. "And what's this 'chain of command' stuff? What's a 'support staff'?"

Sometimes the biggest surprise for rookies is the discovery that contributing to a team effort is a critical factor in personal career success. Yes, you may have met a few of your future team members during the interview process, but that seemed like a formality. Now suddenly you find that being likable, helpful, enthusiastic, and outgoing are going to be pretty important to your initial success. "Whoa! I'm a charter member of the Lone Wolf Club," you say. "We don't do this collaboration stuff."

Relax. Despite a few exceptions, corporate teams aren't like the Borg Collective. You'll probably find you have a lot in common with your fellow team members and you'll be working together to achieve similar goals. If you really don't like being part of a well-integrated team, visit Chapter 11 for some help. Otherwise, start with these basic guidelines on how to behave like a good team player:

✓ **Don't brag about your own competence:** If you've made the team — that is, if you've been hired — it's assumed that you're equally as smart as your co-workers (after all, they got hired, too). Unless you're part of a highly-competitive group like sales or R&D, you should never try to score points against your own team mates.

✓ **Take the initiative:** Don't wait to be invited to join the group: Introduce yourself, ask for advice, hang out with co-workers, show interest in their personal lives, do small favors. Wash your own coffee cup in the break room.

✓ **Be trustworthy:** Trust is the glue that keeps organizations together. But for day-to-day interactions among team members, trust usually translates into *being reliable*. Show up for meetings on time, deliver assignments when promised, don't make excuses about "emergencies" that could have been avoided. The whole point of a team effort is close coordination, so any missing player can disrupt everyone's effort. If you can't be trusted to play your part, you'll soon be warming the bench.

✓ **Master the rule book:** Most teams "play by the rules" — every member is expected to follow standard procedures, use shared terms and templates, and pay attention to project plans. As a new employee, one of your top priorities is to learn these rules (often unwritten) so you can interact smoothly with other team members. Moreover, teams tend to take their rules very seriously. If you've ever watched a judge browbeat an inexperienced attorney over basic courtroom procedures, you've witnessed what can happen to even the most innocent rule-breaker.

✓ **Show respect for the team's expertise:** As a newcomer, you may see (or think you see) better ways to do the team's job. But for now, just sit quietly and watch. If something doesn't seem to make sense, ask for an explanation — respectfully. Never imply that a wet-behind-the-ears newbie like yourself can see what the veterans were too oblivious to notice.

✓ **Avoid negativity:** Your team members will probably complain about their jobs, their managers, a lazy co-worker, their paychecks, their family members, and the company's lousy products. However, all of these topics are off-limits for you during your early days as an employee. Once you've demonstrated that you're a loyal and trustworthy team member, you can be as critical as you want. Until then, the team may see your negativity as evidence that you're not a team player.

✓ **Show respect for the team's diversity:** Peter Drucker points out that members of most working teams "are as much individuals as you yourself are. They perversely insist on behaving like human beings... each works his or her way, not your way."

What matters is whether they perform and what their values are. As for how they perform—each is likely to do it differently. The first secret of effectiveness is to understand the people you work with and depend on so that you can make use of their strengths, their ways of working, and their values.

✓ **Remember names:** In your first few weeks on the job, you'll meet literally dozens of people who will become part of your working world. Take notes immediately on each person you meet (especially your team members), organize the names by department or role, and later fill in relevant background material from LinkedIn or Facebook. And make sure you have a company org chart. That's your map to how the company is organized, top to bottom, side to side.

✓ **Share the glory:** Carnegie Mellon professor Robert Kelley has done extensive work with companies that are eager to cultivate star performers, and he's discovered that the best performers are careful to share credit with their fellow team members:

> In an economy where knowledge is the stock in trade of so many businesses, there are no reputations worse than being pegged as an idea thief, as a pseudo-star who stands on stage and acts as if there were no supporting players, or as a taker who doesn't reciprocate. These behaviors relegate workers far beyond the average ranks to the small minority that no one wants to work with.

★

Four Kinds of Teams

"I have a problem," says one reader. "I've been comparing notes with my friends, and we're all surprised by the differences in the so-called teams we see in our new jobs. I work for a building contractor who pulls together a bunch of us for each gig he gets (sometimes including subcontractors who don't even work for our company). A friend of mine works in a fast-food restaurant where he says 'there are more handoffs and rules than in a basketball game.' Another friend works in

the post office sorting mail, and she says she barely talks to the other clerks who are doing the same job.

"I think we'd all like to do well as 'team players,' but are we even playing the same game?"

Yes, in many important ways, you and your friends are working together to deliver results that you probably couldn't achieve as individuals — building a house, feeding a hundred people, delivering thousands of letters. The details may vary, but your success depends on how well the whole team works together.

But even in the world of team sports (the favorite example of management gurus and academics) there's a difference between a baseball team and a basketball team. Soccer teams aren't like cricket teams, volleyball isn't hockey, and an Olympic relay race may involve precision handoffs that the fans can barely detect.

And these differences have an impact on who's a "star" player.

Since you're part of a construction team, take a look at how other contractors manage their teams. The odds are that almost everyone *in your industry* works pretty much the same way: They create teams for each major project, and then reassign those team members to the next big job that comes along... or maybe to some smaller jobs if nothing big is on the schedule. This kind of project-based teamwork puts a high value on employees who can be flexible, who have a variety of skills, and who don't need strict rules or close supervision. For most businesses that specialize in project work, this seems to be the formula that simply works best.

Meanwhile, other industries have found how to win with different kinds of teamwork. Your restaurant friend, for instance, works in a business where good teamwork is defined largely by delivering *consistency* — a meal that reaches the customer exactly on time, exactly as promised in the menu. And your friend in the post office is probably part of a unionized team that (for better or worse) defines teamwork in terms of strict production quotas and contract terms.

In short, the trick to "doing well as a team player" is to start by understanding how the game is played in your particular industry... and to figure out why this specific approach seems to be a practical solution.

You might also want to look at other kinds of businesses that work the same way as yours, because you might pick up a few useful insights. Your friend in the post office has a job that's pretty similar to the assembly line that Henry Ford used to build the famous Model T auto; your own construction teams look remarkably like the teams that an ad agency assigns to a client's advertising campaign; your restaurant buddy would be right at home in a surgical ward or a daily newspaper.

In case you're curious about these similarities, we've put together the following summary of four common team models. (It's rather dense reading, so feel free to skip this section. No offense taken.)

A Typology of Teams
....

Type #1: Closed Teams: These are the teams that look the most like professional basketball or football teams. Closed teams are usually strictly organized, with well-defined membership and smooth handoffs among team members. A strong top-level leader usually controls how tasks will be performed. Rules, checklists and "playbook" procedures are important; there is usually a sense of urgency about meeting deadlines or delivering results; and management pays considerable attention to the team's collective "score" or similar performance metrics.

Examples: Hospitals, manufacturing plants, restaurant kitchens, airline cockpits, daily newspapers, large-scale retail, military teams.

Employee Culture: Little staff turnover, but some upward mobility within the team based on additional training or skills. Job descriptions and titles tend to be formal and standardized. Status is based on a combination of factors, including performance, seniority, and sometimes public recognition. Team members have low tolerance for "lone wolf" employees and innovations that might upset well-practiced procedures.

....

31

Type #2: Open Teams: Open teams are common whenever a team's core members are professionals or experts who work largely as individual specialists — lawyers, academics, accountants, management consultants, and the like. Open teams are also common in smaller businesses that are managed by a single founder (and spouse). The team is usually loosely structured around the talents of individual members, with a minimum of rules or standard procedures. Senior team members play a large role in managing the team's business, though ongoing administrative tasks may be assigned to a managing partner with relatively limited authority. Success is measured largely in terms of revenue contributions and major individual accomplishments — for instance, new client recruitment, publications, grants, awards, courtroom success.

> *Examples:* Law offices, college faculty departments, management consulting groups, financial and investment firms, research laboratories, barber shops and beauty salons, smaller retail and service businesses.

> *Employee Culture:* Little staff turnover or upward mobility; often a rigid social divide between professionals or owners and the support staff. Minimal bureaucracy and considerable tolerance for high-performing "lone wolf" employees (who may even be independent contractors), but usually conservative about innovations that might take attention off the team's primary work.

....

Type #3: Project Teams: Project teams are usually assembled from a pool of permanent staff plus outside talent for a well-defined project or major account. Roles are largely defined by the specific needs of the project, and the details of implementation are usually overseen by a core group of managers and senior specialists who have worked together before. Success is typically measured in terms of budget and frequent project milestones, as well as the quality of the completed project.

> *Examples:* Advertising and public relations agencies, building contractors, IT departments, political campaigns, Hollywood film producers.

> *Employee Culture:* Staff is recruited only for the life of the project, or even for part of that period. There is almost no job mobility while the project is under way, but success may lead to subsequent promotions. The work environment is democratic and results-oriented; status usually reflects talent and reputation. "Lone wolf" employees are welcome, but managers tend to be conservative about introducing distracting innovations.

Type #4: Assembly Line Teams: Like their factory namesakes, assembly line teams have minimal interaction among members. They perform repetitive tasks that are generally part of a standard process for handling documents, customer calls, or financial transactions. Employee roles and performance standards are largely defined by management playbooks and union contracts, and the team's own manager or supervisor may have little discretion over how work is performed. Success is measured largely in terms of total tasks performed (number of documents, calls, transactions, etc.).

Examples: Large-scale manufacturing, insurance claims processing, order fulfillment, legal document review, call centers, fast-food restaurant service.

Employee Culture: Staff turnover may be high, often creating openings for rapid promotions; occasional layoffs may occur during low-volume periods. Little social interaction while on the job, but usually friendly social relationships after work. "Lone wolf" employees are welcome as long as they meet job standards; innovations may be welcome if they promise big efficiency gains.

Committees, Task Forces, and the Inner Circle

If you show signs of talent, there's a good chance you'll be invited to join a special committee or task force. These groups are usually a response to a fairly complex short-term problem — for instance, a multi-department Web site makeover, an office relocation, new performance metrics — and the group dissolves once the problem is solved. Typically, membership is open-ended, there's little synergy among members, and leadership is minimal. If you're well-organized and responsible, you'll probably end up doing a lot of the group's work out of sheer frustration.

The one big personal benefit to serving on a temporary committee is visibility. You'll rub shoulders with people from other parts of the company, and the project itself is likely to have a high profile. Do a good job and you'll be noticed.

You're less likely to join an "inner circle" in your first hundred days, but it does happen on a temporary basis. Most bosses put together an informal group of advisors and friends they use as a sounding board for tough decisions. These groups don't show up in the official company org chart, and often their long-time members are outsiders — lawyers, accountants, spouses, a trusted vendor, maybe a board member. Your own boss may invite you to join his inner circle when he or she is looking for experience in an area where you have special competence — say, setting up a company blog or breaking into a culturally sensitive ethnic market. Be as helpful as you can, and after the problem has been resolved don't be offended when you're not offered a permanent seat at the boss's monthly poker game.

Remember also that *everything* about the boss's inner circle is off limits for discussion with your colleagues. No bragging, no gossip, no leaks about upcoming decisions. Period.

Shared Knowledge

Why do some teams consistently outperform their rivals? Talented players make a big difference, of course. But we tend to overlook a significant intangible asset — the team's *shared knowledge*.

For instance: A winning sports team will have a closely-guarded playbook filled with tactics that the team has tested and practiced. Lawyers have whole libraries of law books filled with interpretations of esoteric rules and winning arguments. Engineers have materials handbooks, tech support departments have online knowledgebases, auto mechanics have manufacturers' repair manuals, sales teams have contract templates and customer histories... the examples go on almost without end.

In fact, most companies are up to their eyeballs in shared knowledge. Much of this knowledge is informal — a purchasing department's knowledge of which vendors are reliable, a marketing group's knowledge of how its customers respond to surveys, an accounting department's knowledge of how to lay out an idiot-proof invoice. Little is written down: veteran employees simply know what works and what doesn't work.

And that's often a problem for new team members.

As a rookie, you may discover that shared knowledge isn't always... shared. The veterans on your new team may know hundreds of useful tips and techniques, but *finding* that knowledge can take a good deal of effort. According to Phil Verghis, a developer of knowledge management tools, "the average worker spends 20% of their work week looking for internal information or tracking down colleagues who can help." Verghis also points out that team members usually have little incentive to make their knowledge easier to access. "You have to address the question of 'What's in it for me? Why should I share information if all you're going to do is eliminate or outsource my job?'"

If you run into pushback when you try to access your team's secret wisdom, these tips may be helpful:

✓ **Be a great listener:** No surprise — often, the best ice-breaker is simply to show an active interest in what a co-worker is saying. Says Michelle Lederman, author of *The 11 Laws of Likability*: "As an effective listener, you will establish stronger connections with the people you engage, you'll have a more robust understanding of what is being said, and you'll get more out of conversations." Resist the temptation to show your fellow team members how much you know: instead, let them show off their knowledge. You'll open the floodgates.

✓ **Make friends with the old-timers:** Pay special attention to long-time employees who are usually the keepers of what's called "institutional memory." They can probably tell you *why* the company operates in a particular way, and how its landmark successes came about.

✓ **Don't overlook public sources:** A good deal of useful knowledge can be found in company histories, online forums, customer databases, and public financial reports. You may not find the behind-the-scenes details, but it's easier to get your team members to share those details if you seem to understand the big picture.

✓ **Identify the team specialists:** "Knowledge leadership comes in many forms," says Carnegie Mellon's Robert Kelley. "Some people have amazing expertise in a specific field; others are experts in processes – they know how to work the system."

> Still others are expert practitioners of perspective... Perspective knowledge leaders can play the current game, but they also understand how the game and its rules are changing. They are known to have good instincts and intuition – their hunches are often right on target.

✓ **Become the go-to expert for knowledge sharing:** Volunteer to build document templates, map procedures, organize files, and edit knowledgebase articles. Investigate new systems for managing information about customers and responding to lookup requests. Update your team's playbook (formal or informal) to streamline the team's workflow and produce better, faster results.

★

Dysfunctional Teams

"I've been assigned to an account team that does nothing but fight," a reader says. *"I don't have a lot of experience with teams, but my colleagues are constantly bickering and undercutting each other, sometimes in front of clients. I certainly can't see any group synergy with this group – we'd be better off working solo."*

Sadly, your experience isn't unusual.

You'd expect that the enormous popularity of team sports in our culture would teach a few lessons about how make a team successful. Yet somehow all the armchair analysis of team performance doesn't seem to prevent a near-epidemic of dysfunctional teams even in well-managed companies.

36

"Research consistently shows that teams underperform, despite all the extra resources they have," says J. Richard Hackman, a professor of social and organizational psychology at Harvard University who has spent years studying "the wisdom of teams." His depressing conclusion: "Problems with coordination and motivation typically chip away at the benefits of collaboration. Having a team is often worse than having no team at all."

What are the symptoms of teams that are in trouble? Professor Hackman recently shared some observations with Diane Coutu, a senior editor at the Harvard Business Review:

On fuzzy team boundaries: Common sense suggests that "Who's on my team?" should be a simple question to answer, says Hackman. "Yet when we asked members [of more than 120 teams of senior executives] to describe their team, fewer than 10% agreed about who was on it!" Hackman points out that it's a boss's job to figure out who belongs on the team—and who doesn't.

> We worked with a large financial services firm where the CFO wasn't allowed on the executive committee because he was clearly a team destroyer. He was disinclined toward teamwork, he was unwilling to work at finding collective solutions, and every team he was on got in trouble. The CEO invited the CFO to stay in his role because he was a truly able executive, but he was not allowed on the senior executive team.

If you can't seem to get a straight answer about who's actually on your new team, be especially careful about who gets invited to meetings (that includes you, by the way), who gets copied on emails and reports, and who has the authority to approve changes and exceptions to team rules. If in doubt, ask a veteran team member to warn you about potentially awkward situations.

On an absence of compelling direction: You can't have a successful team without an explicit team goal, says Hackman. "Setting a direction is emotionally demanding because it always involves the exercise of authority," he points out, "and that inevitably arouses angst and ambivalence—for both the person exercising it and the people on the receiving end. A leader sometimes encounters resistance so intense that it can place his or her job at risk."

For team members, lack of strong leadership can trigger a low-key war of competing agendas, he adds. Avoid taking sides if you can: there's little benefit to being a winner, and lots of career risk if you end up on the losing side.

On too many team members: Would a baseball team win more games with 18 players on the field at a time? Probably not. Hackman argues that big teams ("my rule of thumb is no double digits") have so much trouble coordinating with each other that "they usually wind up just wasting everybody's time." (Incidentally, Amazon CEO Jeff Bezos has a similar "two-pizza" rule: "If it takes more than two pizzas to feed the team, the team is too big.")

You'll notice that most teams that *seem* to be large—a sales department, for instance, or a call center—really operate as much smaller sub-teams whose day-to-day work is managed by supervisors or team leaders. That's who's really in charge.

On a lack of team experience: Especially when smooth handoffs and tight coordination are critical, team members are likely to fumble if they haven't worked together before. The problem isn't a lack of talent or skill, says Hackman—it's that people who work together for long periods of time develop specific team skills.

> Consider crews flying commercial airplanes. The National Transportation Safety Board found that 73% of the incidents in its database occurred on a crew's first day of flying together, before people had the chance to learn through experience how best to operate as a team—and 44% of those took place on a crew's very first flight.

Pay special attention to how team members interact with each other. Do your colleagues seem to trust each other? Do they follow directions exactly or do they get creative? Are you sometimes surprised by what the rest of the team is doing? Hmm...

On too much consensus: Despite the importance of smooth interaction, says Hackman, many teams eventually become stale and complacent. That's when they need a member who acts as a "deviant" — "someone who can help the team by challenging the tendency to want too much homogeneity, which can stifle creativity and learning."

> In our research, we've looked carefully at both teams that produced something original and those that were merely average, where nothing really sparkled. It turned out that the teams with deviants outperformed teams without them. In many cases, deviant thinking is a source of great innovation.

But don't be too eager to take on the deviant role. Hackman points out that questioning popular wisdom can be dangerous, particularly for newbie team members. "Many team leaders crack down on deviants and try to get them to stop asking difficult questions, and maybe even knock them off the team."

CHAPTER 4

Relationships: Your Network

"Inside every working anarchy, there's an Old Boy Network."
— Mitchell Kapor

To job hunters, "networking" is an informal way to generate job leads and referrals. It mostly involves hit-or-miss interactions between people who are usually strangers, with perhaps some tenuous point of connection. "Josie! I don't really remember you, but weren't we both at the Harvard-Yale football game four years ago? Let's have coffee and trade business cards!"

The business networks you develop in your new job are going to be much more valuable than just trading business cards.

Almost always, business networks consist of people who have actual relationships with each other. They have real shared interests — as co-workers, buyers and sellers, members of the same industry or profession, or as other kinds of stakeholders in your new company's business.

Typically, these informal "shadow" networks exist alongside the company's formal hierarchy of executives and managers. In fact, many of the most powerful members of the shadow network world are the admin assistants who serve as gatekeepers to top management. If a gatekeeper likes you, you'll get on the boss's calendar. If you behave badly, you become a non-person.

You won't see these networks on a company org chart, but shadow networks play a key role in how the business operates at a more granular level. They are literally "how things get done."

Building your own shadow network (or joining existing networks) can be especially important if you end up working for a company that's become bureaucratic, inefficient, or strangled by its own rules and procedures. If it takes weeks to process simple paperwork or make an appointment with your boss, if getting the copier fixed takes three executive signatures, if customers are ticked off about unresponsive service — you need to start building an internal network of friends who are willing to help out. And you need to start building your network right away.

Networks are also valuable during the inevitable moments of company conflict and stress. Here's how Dr. Marie McIntyre, an organizational psychologist, describes the payoff from investing in building a personal network:

> Highly task-driven people often see interpersonal interaction as an unnecessary distraction from 'real' work. What they fail to realize is that some of those distracting relationships might actually help them produce better results. When some unexpected catastrophe forces those reclusive souls to communicate with long-ignored associates, conflicts often erupt. Without an established relationship, people quickly start blaming and faultfinding, thereby reducing both the likelihood of solving the immediate problem and the odds of any positive communication in the future. A history of friendly interaction always helps to buffer the unavoidable stresses that accompany a crisis.

Finally, you'll also need a broad network of people *outside* the company who can give you advice and feedback. What's really on the minds of your customers and clients? Where is your industry headed? Who has hands-on experience with new technologies or vendors that you're considering? You won't find the answers by chatting with your co-workers in the company cafeteria...

But why should these folks help you?

One obvious reason is the hope that you'll do favors for them in return. That's the first rule of networking — help the people who help you. (This is also known as "The Godfather Rule": As Don Corleone says after helping a family member, "Some day, and that day may never come, I will call upon you to do a service for me.")

But it's not likely that a newly-hired employee will be in a position to grant favors to friends. In fact, don't even try: You'll need lots of experience to know how to bend company rules or share corporate intelligence.

Instead, according to Dale Carnegie, the legendary author of *How to Win Friends and Influence People*, you can make people feel good about themselves. One of the most powerful forces that drives human behavior, Carnegie once said, is "a feeling of importance":

> There is one longing—almost as deep, almost as imperious, as the desire for food or sleep—which is seldom gratified. It is what Freud calls 'the desire to be great.' It is what Dewey calls the 'desire to be important.' ... The rare individual who honestly satisfies this heart hunger will hold people in the palm of his or her hand.

Think about Carnegie's point for a minute or so. We do feel good—often very good—when someone thanks us for a small favor. We're impressed by thank-you notes, small gifts, follow-up letters, even a big smile. We're impressed when someone *listens* to our opinion and advice. We love applause, public credit, and the secret knowledge that we influenced something big.

Recognition seems obviously important, yet it's surprisingly rare in most big, impersonal companies. As a result, many employees end up feeling unappreciated. And corporate impersonality usually extends beyond the company itself, to customers, vendors, and even investors. If you can break through the impersonality and show genuine appreciation and interest, you'll quickly build a highly effective personal network.

A few networking guidelines for building an internal network:

✓ **Don't start by asking for a favor:** Introduce yourself ("I'm the new kid in the traffic department"), preferably in a social setting or at a lunch break. Show sincere interest in your subject's job, background, and opinions. Smile a lot and sound enthusiastic about your new company. Never mention the topic of favors or influence: you should show interest in the individual ("Margaret Kline"), not their job description ("executive assistant to the vice president").

✓ **Never brag about your access:** A network is not about your ability to manipulate people. "I managed to convince Hank from IT to come in at 7:00am to fix our projector" makes you sound like you pulled rank. However, giving credit is fine: "I'd especially like to thank Hank for last-minute projector fixes in time for our big presentation." This way, Hank looks like the hero.

✓ **Be a fan:** Show up at company baseball games, concerts where department members are performing, and press conferences. This is a hugely powerful show of your interest, and it will definitely be noticed.

✓ **Avoid flattery:** Sincerity is hard to fake. Dale Carnegie makes a good point about sounding too appreciative: "In the long run, flattery will do you no good. Flattery is counterfeit, and like counterfeit money it will eventually get you into trouble."

✓ **Avoid toxic people:** "We all know who they are," says motivation expert Chester Elton. "There's typically a group of people who complain about everything at the office. If the boss pulls out her wallet and starts handing out twenty-dollar bills, the whiners will later moan that they weren't fifties." Don't join a social network that includes these people, and don't encourage them to join your network. Their negativism will make it hard to achieve any positive team results.

★

Managing Your Mentor

Mentoring is one of those odd human relationships that's remarkably hard to define. Being a mentor usually isn't a job title or even part of a formal job description; most mentors are essentially just friends (typically older and more experienced) who offer advice about your career. In return, mentors get... what? Satisfaction, gratitude, interesting conversation, perhaps a chance to guide a future star. In the end, a mentoring relationship usually depends more on personal chemistry than anything else.

Nebulous or not, mentoring relationships can be extraordinarily valuable to a new employee. Lee Iacocca, one of the auto industry's most influential chief executives, says an early mentor inspired insights that ultimately helped shape his whole leadership strategy: "A guy named Charlie Beacham was my first mentor at Ford," Iacocca recalls. "He taught me the importance of the dealers, and he rubbed my nose in the retail business."

In fact, a few companies have tried to incorporate mentoring assignments into their onboarding programs for new employees. At Morgan Stanley, for instance, a special mentoring track helps new female employees succeed in the finance industry's traditionally male-dominated culture. But more commonly, mentoring relationships spring up spontaneously. Some mentors are simply veteran employees or mid-level managers; others may be consultants, lawyers, financial advisors, investors, perhaps a vendor (a risky mentoring relationship), or maybe a long-time client.

Moreover, there's rarely any formal agenda to a mentoring relationship—no performance metrics or responsibilities on either side. You may simply hang out with your mentor as you would with any friend. Or you can set up a more structured relationship, such as an annual review of your career highlights. Whatever works.

Some guidelines for a successful mentoring relationship:

 Be a good friend: Show gratitude for the advice and support you're getting, be accessible whenever your mentor wants to get together, and try to hold up your end of the conversation (no whining about how life is unfair). If your mentor makes a recommendation, listen carefully. Your mentor's advice may sound nutty, but remember that he or she knows a lot more than you do.

✓ **Don't ask for more than advice:** As a general rule, mentors aren't expected to write letters of recommendation, generate sales leads, invest in startups, land jobs for your friends, or provide free professional services. Ross McCammon says that even asking for help with a tough decision is likely to be off limits. "Offering a recommendation involves analysis and decision-making. Decisions are hard. Decisions are work."

Of course, your mentors may *volunteer* to do any of these things — but they should be the first to raise the issue.

✓ **Be careful about gossip:** Inevitably, your conversations will touch on personalities in the company, questionable decisions, and other sensitive topics. Especially if your mentor is an outsider, you have no guarantee that your comments will stay confidential. And your mentor won't be happy to find that you've shared his unflattering opinion of a colleague with your co-workers. Loose lips sink ships.

★

Customers and Vendors

In popular mythology, vendors and their customers live in a world of perpetual struggle. Every purchase supposedly involves fights over pricing and competitive alternatives. Customers endlessly demand more than they paid for, while vendors do their best to cut corners.

But that's the overhyped soap opera version.

Yes, competition for big deals is sometimes intense. And yes, there are crooks and scam artists who prey on the unsuspecting. Stay out of dark alleys and don't believe in free lunches.

However, the vast majority of business relationships are pretty cozy. Over time, you'll discover that buyers and sellers learn to trust each other, and surprisingly often they rely on each other for advice, referrals, and industry know-how. If you can plug into your company's network of customers and vendors, you'll add valuable resources to your personal network.

How do you start? Some tips:

✓ **First, figure out who's who:** Look particularly for people who seem to enjoy being helpful — regular contributors on industry-specific online forums, members of your company's advisory board, consultants, workshop instructors, conference speakers. Some of these people will try to sell you their services; others will be too busy to invest time in a brand-new employee. But at least a few will be happy to share their expertise with a willing listener. And a very few will become real friends.

✓ **Get permission to contact your prospects:** Discuss the ground rules with your boss. Many companies frown on unapproved contacts with customers and vendors, and there may be some history you ought to know about (that prolific forum contributor may have insulted your CEO; the charming consultant will send a bill for every minute you're on the phone). Offer to write up a memo for your boss for every conversation you have — that's likely to be valuable feedback that will make your networking efforts sound more useful.

✓ **Stay away from pricing discussions:** Yes, everyone loves to talk about prices and pricing models. But the rule is simple: Don't go there. Vendors and customers will use any scrap of information you give them to negotiate better deals, enraging your sales reps and purchasing agents. And if you talk to someone who works for a competitor — even a very indirect competitor — a conversation about pricing *might* violate anti-trust laws. If it's a group discussion, leave the room and get caught up on your email somewhere else. This is serious stuff.

✓ **Learn to listen:** When you get together to chat, remember that you're not making a sales call. Just ask open-ended questions: "How can we do a better job for you?" "What are other companies doing that you wish we'd do?" "Are there any bottlenecks that make it hard to do business with us?" Stay away from product issues, personalities, and your company's deceptive advertising (that's up to the sales force to handle).

✓ **Make friends with the customer's support staff:** "Respect everyone," says author Clinton Greenleaf. "It's a great help to have an extra cheerleader in your camp," he adds, especially when you're developing relationships with clients or other influential outsiders.

> Never underestimate the number of times you will have to call a client needing to speak about an important issue and be at the mercy of his or her staff. If you have a good relationship with the staff, many more doors will open and more opportunities will become available.

✓ **Keep the relationship alive:** If someone has been particularly helpful, look for ways to build on your first meeting. Of course, you should send a thank-you note... but also stay in touch on an occasional basis. Get together at trade shows and conferences, send an article or book that you think would be interesting, perhaps recommend your new contact for a company advisory board slot. Best of all, if your company implements a suggestion that came out of your initial discussions, let your networking friend know right away. Giving bragging rights to a helper are a priceless way to say Thank You.

✓ **Develop a "Top Contacts" list:** Tim Sanders, the author of *The Likeability Factor*, says it's often a good idea to create a special "frequent contact circle" list of key people in your network. Don't just rely on random email contacts with this group, Sanders says. Instead, "warm up your channel of communication" by making regular phone calls or even arranging face-to-face meetings:

Email is the coldest form of communication. It sends the fewest cues, communicates the fewest emotions, and produces the lowest-quality contact. You will seldom be relevant to someone if all your contact is through email... Find a way to pick up the phone at the very least once a month and have a conversation. You can establish relevance through happiness, laughter. sadness, and all the other voice-expressed emotions.

Social Media Relationships

As any self-respecting Millennial will tell you, we live in a digital world where "everybody" connects through social media. But here's the bad news: It's very possible that hardly anyone is listening to you. "Quit assuming that tools create connections," warns Jeff Haden:

> Twitter followers, Facebook friends, and LinkedIn connections are great — if those connections are in some way active and engaged. But in all likelihood your Twitter followers aren't reading your tweets. Your Facebook friends rarely visit your page. Your LinkedIn connections aren't constantly scanning for your updates.

No surprise: social media relationships work pretty much like old-fashioned friendships, but with fewer constraints of geography and time. If you're fascinated by Japanese spider charts, for instance, you might have trouble finding even one local friend who wants to chat — but you can probably put together a *virtual* worldwide network of like-minded Spider chart enthusiasts. And the same holds true for almost any subject you can imagine. That kind of network really is priceless... and you can often draw on these relationships if you're looking for help with a knotty work problem.

Some guidelines:

 Connect with your peers: Try to find networking connections who are at roughly the same point in their careers as you are, and in similar jobs. They'll almost certainly relate to your personal issues more deeply than your cousin the transcontinental trucker or your neighbor who's a corporate vice-president. And don't waste time trying to connect with celebrities, billionaires, or industry luminaries. You may get a polite response, but that's not the same as a sustained networking relationship.

✓ **Avoid zombie hangouts:** Vast numbers of online communities on LinkedIn and Facebook have impressive membership counts and postings. But if you look closely, you'll sometimes notice an absence of any *interactive* discussions. These sites usually exist for promotional purposes (typically links to other blogs and vanity articles). Don't try to strike up a conversation — nobody's home.

✓ **Stay visible:** If you want people to remember you, you *must* keep up the conversation with reasonable frequency. Fortunately, you'll be competing for attention against people who think that the world will notice their one tweet a month or their occasional comment in a LinkedIn forum. And try to say things that are memorable. Just agreeing with everyone else is a one-way ticket to invisibility.

A good way to increase your visibility, incidentally, is to take advantage of YouTube and other online video channels. Volunteer to act as a narrator for your company's webcasts, training videos, online demos, tech support and how-to videos, and marketing announcements. If you're good, pretty soon you'll become a semi-celebrity. People will ask you, "Hey, don't I know you from somewhere?" Just smile.

✓ **Help others first:** The most annoying would-be networkers are people who only surface every few years to beg for job leads or other favors. Author Mark Babbitt says a far better networking approach is to become what he calls a "relentless giver" — "that person who shares consistently, goes out of their way to introduce others, and answers the call when friends need help."

Yes, this takes some work... but the rewards are well worth the effort. Why? Because when a Relentless Giver finally asks for help, everyone wants to reciprocate. Need an introduction to an influencer? A lead on a new job? Launching a podcast or a e-book? Your personal brand is well-respected... and your network is ready to assist.

✓ **Monitor your digital personality:** Most social media channels will let you collect and review your own postings. Every few months, it's a good idea to review what you've been telling your network friends about yourself. Do you come across as harsh and judgmental? Are your comments hard to figure out? Too personal? A bit longwinded? Remember, your postings are essentially the only clues that you provide online about who you are. If you sound like a jerk, that's what your friends will remember.

Results

By the time you start looking for your first job, you've probably spent most of your life learning new skills. You can solve equations, speak French, tune an engine, write HTML code, draft a legal brief, or lay out a sales brochure.

But here's the hard truth: All the effort and cash you spent to master these skills accomplished just one thing: **They got your foot in the door.**

What you'll eventually discover is that your new employers have a different perspective on skills than you do. To them, your skills are just a starting point for meaningful work. Skills enable you to perform essential tasks and deliver valuable results. You'll collect a paycheck for accomplishing those tasks and results. But sadly, you'll get few rewards just for *having* a great portfolio of skills.

Understanding this new perspective can be tricky, because your boss and other managers will probably talk a fair amount about training and skills development during your first weeks on the job. But their focus isn't academic: They want you to become more productive, to use your skills to achieve company goals.

In the following three chapters, you'll discover how your new company defines, measures, and prioritizes the results you're expected to deliver. And you'll see how focusing on these results will help you position yourself as a star performer, ready to rise quickly and earn the most desirable assignments and clients.

CHAPTER 5

Results: Tasks vs. Results

"People don't want to buy a quarter-inch drill.
They want a quarter-inch hole."
—Theodore Levitt

Chances are, you were hired to do a pretty specific job. Your job description says you're a programmer, an event planner, a sales rep... perhaps a call center supervisor, an auto mechanic, or a bookkeeper.

But your job description almost certainly doesn't tell you one crucial piece of information: Why does your job exist in the first place?

"That's because the answer is obvious," you say. "The company needs programmers, event planners, sales reps, and all those other people. You couldn't have a company without people to do these jobs."

Well, not exactly.

What companies need are the *results* of the tasks that their employees perform—for instance, revenues, new products, services to customers, and profits for investors. Hiring employees like you is simply one way to make these results happen.

Marketing guru Theodore Levitt made this point back in 1983, in a landmark book called *The Marketing Imagination* that helped transform the way business managers think. "People don't want to buy a quarter-inch drill," Levitt pointed out. "They want a quarter-inch hole."

The same results-oriented principle holds true for most jobs: Companies don't create job openings so they can have a programmer, an event planner, or a sales rep on the payroll. They hire people because a decision-maker said, "Hey, we need to get something done here. Let's hire a body to make it happen."

In other words, your new job exists because the company needs some kind of **specific results.**

Sounds like a simple idea, no? In fact, for most simple jobs, the connection between an employee's job description and the desired results is quite clear. A toll collector takes coins from drivers and makes change. A dish washer produces clean dishes. An order entry clerk types data into a computer. Like Levitt's famous quarter-inch drill, these jobs exist because they satisfy a direct, easy-to-understand need.

However... jobs that deliver single, simple results like these are fairly rare. That's because it's often inefficient to use full-time employees for basic, repetitious tasks — and deadly dull for the employee. No surprise: These jobs also tend to be the first to be eliminated by automation or outsourcing.

When Jobs Become More Complex

More commonly, full-time jobs involve a mix of tasks. For instance, an office manager in a small doctor's office may schedule appointments, greet patients, process insurance claims, order supplies, and update patient records. Taken individually, these are fairly low-value housekeeping tasks. But taken as a whole, these tasks contribute to an important end result — a medical practice that operates in a well-organized, professional fashion. When these tasks are all performed well, the doctor becomes more productive, the practice becomes more profitable, and customers tend to feel a greater sense of trust. That modest-sounding job suddenly becomes a big deal.

And complex multi-tasking jobs typically generate dramatically *bigger* results than single-task jobs. Scott McKelvey, a New Jersey marketing consultant, says he was thinking about Levitt's quarter-inch drill metaphor when he was buying tools for a carpentry project. "When I plunked down my money for a drill, I didn't pay for holes," McKelvey says. "My first major project with the drill was to hang a bunch of shelves, hooks, and racks in the garage. I created massive amounts of storage space. I was able to put boxes and storage bins on the shelves and hang chairs, ladders, yard tools, and hoses on the hooks and racks.

The extra storage space was the end result. That's what I really paid for."

"Massive amounts of storage space"... same quarter-inch drill, but this time the desired outcome was literally *hundreds* of precisely-arranged holes. A more complex project, much bigger results.

> **A good rule of thumb:** Employees who can handle big, complex projects tend to deliver big results. More dollars, higher satisfaction scores, better quality metrics, more lines of code, bigger gains in renewal rates... whatever the results that their jobs are expected to produce, these folks deliver. (Yes, there are exceptions. Your mileage may vary.)

If your goal is to rise through the ranks quickly, you should use your first hundred days to zero in on future assignments that will produce these "big results." As a newbie, you almost certainly won't be given these assignments right away — after all, big, complex projects also have a higher risk of failure. But you can lay the groundwork for higher-impact tasks by demonstrating competence and initiative in handling the work you do in your entry-level phase.

The Underpants Gnomes Business Plan

So how do you demonstrate your ability to produce exceptional results?

That's often a harder question than it seems at first. Consider the "Underpants Gnomes Business Plan" made famous by the TV cartoon show South Park. The underpants gnomes devised an ingenious business plan based on stealing underwear:

> **Phase 1: Collect underpants**
> **Phase 2: ?**
> **Phase 3: Profit**

"Collect underpants" is a task — a job description. "Profit" is the goal — a result. Trouble is, *it's not clear how the task leads to the desired results.* The gnomes can work hard and do a superb job of stealing underwear... but their "business plan" lacks any clue about how this effort translates into the outcome they expect. (If this example sounds fanciful, ask a few venture capitalists how many new business plans they see that reflect an Underpants Gnome-like strategy.)

Like the underpants gnomes, your challenge as a new employee is to make a connection between the day-to-day details of your job with the results you hope to achieve. You can't just leave a question mark as your answer to "how will I make these results happen?"

You may also need to figure out what the *company's* priorities are, especially if you're not clear about the various kinds of goals that companies seem to pursue. (See Chapters 6 and 7 for more on this subject.) Some companies simply want to generate piles of cash; others focus on quality, innovation, happy customers, asset values, or a stellar reputation. Working hard to achieve the wrong results is not a smart career move.

In fact, figuring out how to achieve multiple goals — some of which may conflict with each other — is often the toughest part of a complex job. You'll need to become a master organizer and time manager to get everything done, and you'll need to understand how to set the "right" priorities — that is, priorities that deliver the results that your boss and other stakeholders think are important.

Some examples:

Gertrude the event planner was hired to organize an annual conference for her company's clients. Gertrude was given a checklist of logistical tasks to manage, but she never thought to ask what her company was trying to achieve by producing the conference. Was the goal big profits? Visibility for top management? Face-to-face meetings with influential clients? Gertrude figured she'd be safe if she focused on the bottom line. "I didn't have time to invite the press to our CEO's keynote and I cut way back on those boring user group sessions," she reported after the event. "But our profit margins were better than ever!" Oops. Wrong results. Gertrude will soon be moving on.

Scott the programmer's first assignment was to rigorously test a new upgrade of his company's accounting product. "Our last release was so buggy that we lost major clients," Scott's boss warned him. "That can't happen again." But the other programmers in Scott's team told him that their bonuses depended on shipping the software on time, which wouldn't happen if they had to fix a lot of bugs. "Help! I'm stuck in the middle," Scott told his boss. "I can give you software that's bug-free or software that's on time, but not both."

Hank the sales rep's job description said that "closing sales" should be his primary goal. But the company also wanted its sales reps to engage customers and promote follow-on visits to the showroom. Hank's weekly sales numbers were about average, but his sales manager noticed that Hank had been building a loyal following of customers who trusted Hank's advice and didn't nitpick on price. Looking more closely, Hank's manager found that Hank consistently generated higher profits – a major corporate goal – than anyone else on the sales team. Soon, Hank found himself promoted to a lead sales job for one of the company's flagship products.

How the Stars Achieve Top Results

As you might expect, plenty of experts have studied top performers to figure out the secrets of their success. The stakes are high: The average company spends upwards of one-fifth of each new employee's salary on recruiting and training costs, and yet only a small fraction of new hires end up delivering exceptional results. In Garrison Keillor's legendary Lake Wobegon, "all the women are strong, all the men are good looking, and all the children are above average." In much of the working world, however, the numbers seem to get turned upside-down: Only a small fraction of new recruits emerge as star material; the rest are at best adequate for their entry-level jobs and often nearly useless for any more demanding role.

In fairness, most companies don't challenge their new recruits to produce exceptional results. The company's early-stage emphasis is typically on learning the basics: mastering standard tasks, sharpening skills, fitting into the company culture. Expectations tend to be higher for more experienced hires –

managers, executives, senior staff – but even then the bar is often set pretty low. As Woody Allen famously remarked, "Eighty percent of success is showing up."

But here's the rarely-mentioned secret: Employers dearly love initiative. They may set expectations based on average performance, but (with rare exceptions) employers are delighted to discover an eager-beaver, a future star, an employee with passion and imagination.

Naturally, you won't instantly get a million-dollar discretionary budget to play with just because you're passionate, and you won't get to redesign your new company's product line, advertising, or comp plan by shouting "Pick me! Pick me!" But within the scope of your own tasks, you should be able to demonstrate significantly better results by using a few of the following tactics:

Tactic #1: Work really hard: Your parents probably shared this bit of perennial advice with you, and it's true – sort of. If your peers are putting in 40 hours a week (or less, figuring in water cooler gossip time and Facebook updates), you'll almost certainly generate better results if you work an extra couple of hours per day or part of your weekend – say, an average of maybe 10 more hours a week. That's simple math.

Unfortunately, the same simple math shows that a few extra hours a day will probably get you no more than a 15% to 20% gain in output – usually barely enough for your boss to notice. Worse, continuous hard work is hard to sustain. People who work long hours and weekends tend to burn out. They make sloppy mistakes and have nothing left for the few times when there's a genuine all-hands-on-deck emergency.

Tactic #2: Upgrade your skills: Once you acquire basic proficiency at a job, your productivity usually goes up dramatically. That's especially true of manual work – carpentry, making sandwiches, working on an assembly line – but it also applies to so-called "knowledge work." Learning where to find information, building a network of contacts, mastering complex software tools – all of these skills help you produce job-related results more efficiently and more accurately with the same level of effort you're now spending as a neophyte.

The challenge for new hires is how to *speed up* this learning process. Your company may schedule a few weeks of training for you, but don't stop there. Watch how your co-workers handle their assignments: Ask for tips, best practices, feedback on your own work. Read how-to books, blogs, and articles by the masters in your profession. Take classes in skills that are relevant to your present job (as opposed to skills you might need to land your next job). If your results can be measured in dollars, units, or some other tangible metric, track your results *weekly* and make sure you see a steady upward trend.

Tactic #3: Master your company's "power tools": Most companies invest heavily in tools that are expected to increase employee productivity—software, machines, lab instruments, office automation systems, and so forth. But Singapore-based training analyst Raman K. Attri points out that one-size-fits-all corporate training classes tend to overload employees with irrelevant information and often fail to cover essential job-specific features. The result, he points out, is that much of the value of these "power tools" is never realized. If standard training is inadequate, Attri adds, employees who want to achieve exceptional results will need to take the initiative to "locate the resources they need to create their own learning game plan."

Tactic #4: If possible, feel good about what you're doing: You may have noticed that people can work incredibly hard at tasks they love. We've all seen high school dropouts master thousands of baseball statistics; we've seen others invest hundreds of hours playing videogames, working out at the gym, or practicing to become professional musicians.

Your day job probably isn't nearly as engaging... but take a closer look at what you might accomplish if you felt your work was more meaningful. Chester Elton, author of *What Motivates Me*, says his research teams have found that "when individuals are fulfilled on the job they not only produce higher quality work and a greater output, but also generally earn higher incomes."

The happiest people we found typically focus their work efforts in service of others rather than on self-gain. That may mean they achieve more or sell more or do more because they truly believe in their products or services and genuinely believe they are helping their customers by putting these goods in their hands—versus those who are simply striving to win a deal and cash a paycheck. It's a subtle change in thinking, but it's important.

Another tantalizing research conclusion: Several studies have found that hourly workers—whose pay tends to be directly linked to specific results—tend to be happier than their salaried counterparts. Researchers theorize that the hourly employees usually see the "concrete worth" of their work in every paycheck, while the connection is less clear for salaried employees.

On the other hand, if there's really nothing you find rewarding about the work you do, you're going to have a tough time doing even a mediocre job. In fact, you should think seriously about finding a more rewarding career path (See Chapter 11). Yes, jobs are hard to find these days. But it's even harder to succeed at any task that you truly hate.

Tactic #5: Work smarter: Another alternative to simple hard work is to look for wasted effort, inefficiencies, and obsolete tasks in your present projects. Are you compiling reports and writing newsletters that no one reads? Does your group waste time collecting data no one uses, processing unnecessary approvals that slow down turnaround time, scheduling shifts that don't align with customer traffic, answering routine service questions that could be moved to the Web? Often, small tweaks in these areas can produce astonishing results.

But how often can a brand-new employee discover a way to dramatically improve a company's results? Elliot Weissbluth, who heads an innovative financial services firm, argues that it's a myth that all important ideas are inspired by visionary leaders. "Actually, [many] innovations tend to be very modest, and often not very sexy changes. But, boy, are they powerful," he points out. "The best ideas—true innovations—come from people working around the edges of their expertise. They know enough to be informed but not enough to be constrained by the 'old way' of doing things."

Of course, suggesting changes in well-established company procedures can be politically risky. But as a new employee, you can plausibly ask your boss, "Gosh, isn't there a more efficient way to do this?" without challenging anyone's authority... and you may trigger a change that saves you and your team hundreds of wasted hours a month.

Tactics #6: Become a conduit for new ideas: Companies often hire consultants simply to discover what's happening outside their own offices. As a newcomer, you can credibly deliver a fresh perspective by paying attention to how your company's competitors and industry leaders handle the same tasks that your own department performs. If you're asked to code a new login page for the company Web site (a pretty mundane task), you could collect examples of a dozen well-implemented login pages from other sites and show them to your boss. Almost certainly, no one bothered to do this work before writing the specs for the new page, so you'll probably be able to suggest a few improvements that will boost traffic counts and satisfaction scores — important results for your department.

Tactic #7: Apply the Pareto Principle: This is the famous "80/20 rule" that reflects the fact that roughly 80% of many kinds of results (e.g., sales, profits, complaints, tech support calls) are often generated by about 20% of customers, employees, products, and other sources. While the exact numbers may vary, the classic "Pareto distribution" is a handy tool for identifying the most productive targets for your efforts. In essence, the Pareto Principle suggests that you should focus your efforts on the 20% that produces the majority of results, rather than waste much time on the 80% that doesn't add much.

In *Low-Hanging Fruit,* authors Jeremy Eden and Terri Long offer a good example of using Pareto analysis to produce big results:

> We know a customer service manager whose team had worked hard on many initiatives to improve their customer satisfaction results, yet without much improvement to show for it. She decided to apply the 80/20 analysis to find the smallest number of

problems that seemed to cause the greatest customer pain. In just a few weeks, she had a list of seven issues that were driving 74% of the complaints. The surprising thing was that several of these issues had never received any attention. For example, it turned out that orders faxed to a communal fax machine were often lost, as other users took them by mistake. The 80/20 analysis revealed the problem and its importance. It also made it simple to think of replacing a paper fax machine with an e-fax phone number. Problem solved — and $250,000 in lost profits recovered!

Tactic #8: Improve your utilization rate: If the results you produce are measured in billable hours or another form of income-producing time, it's likely that your success depends heavily on your "utilization rate" — the percentage of your time that's actually used for serving clients or making sales. With aggressive time management, you can probably nudge your utilization rate up by perhaps ten points — say, from 60% to 70%. That's a big deal in almost any organization.

In particular, look for ways to reduce the time you spend on unnecessary meetings, travel, paperwork, office administration, email, etc., and try to offload low-value tasks to less-expensive support staff or freelancers. If clients are willing to pay you $200 an hour for your services, you probably shouldn't spend your time proofreading proposals or making personal travel arrangements. (Big law firms are particularly aggressive about time management and maximizing billable hours, so you should study their methods for useful insights.)

Tactic #9: Get rid of the junk: Top performers try not to waste time on long-shot deals, troublesome clients, high-risk projects, and other junk work. Instead, they make sure their personal pipeline is stuffed with blue-chip leads and reliable customer relationships. If you don't have enough good leads, you're probably better off working on lead-generation efforts than on chasing marginal accounts.

Most important, says consultant and author Greg McKeown, is simply to learn the power of saying no. "Warren Buffet is credited with having said, 'The difference between successful people and very successful people is that very successful people say no to almost everything.'"

This means, 'Not just haphazardly saying no, but purposefully, deliberately, and strategically eliminating the non-essentials. Not just once a year as part of a planning meeting, but constantly reducing, focusing, and simplifying. Not just getting rid of the obvious time wasters, but being willing to cut out really terrific opportunities as well.'

Tactic #10: Recharge your batteries: According to Tony Schwartz and Catherine McCarthy of the Energy Project, simple lifestyle changes — more sleep, better home life, a healthier diet, brief breaks during the day — can dramatically improve personal performance:

> At Wachovia Bank, we took a group of employees through a pilot [personal] energy management program. The participants outperformed the controls on a series of financial metrics, such as the value of loans they generated. They also reported substantial improvements in their customer relationships, their engagement with work, and their personal satisfaction.

'I Just Want to Do My Job'

"Whoa," says one reader. "This talk about results is way too complicated. I have a detailed job description that doesn't even mention results. Why can't I just do the job I was hired for?"

An excellent question, Grasshopper.

Job descriptions are typically a list of tasks (sometimes called "responsibilities"). Your job description may not even mention results, but results are certainly implied. If you complete these tasks correctly, it's assumed that you'll get the results the company needs.

In fact, there are plenty of people who "just do the job they were hired for." Some of these people deliver great results simply by doing their assigned jobs; others perform tasks that are nice-to-have without being really important. "We've always had three clerks in accounting, so when Frank retired we automatically hired a replacement."

So if you have a well-crafted job description and don't goof off, you're probably home free.

But... there are a couple of pitfalls you should watch out for:

First, you may not understand which tasks are most important. Especially for new employees, it's easy to get sidetracked by low-value tasks that your co-workers have learned to avoid (attending boring committee meetings, drafting reports that no one will read, organizing office parties and baby showers, escorting visiting VIPs on company tours). Everyone will thank you for being a good sport... but when your annual review comes around, your record of *significant* accomplishments will be pretty thin. And over time, your career may drift into dead-end directions that make you expendable. Notice that the star performers in your company always seem to gravitate toward big wins for the company. That's because they know where to focus their efforts.

Second, you'll be at risk whenever your job is re-engineered. Even traditional low-tech businesses are rapidly transforming how they operate. Family farms are becoming integrated agribusinesses, brick-and-mortar retailers are turning into online merchants, schools are becoming remote learning centers... on and on. In fact, two British economists recently concluded that 47% of current jobs are "at high risk of being automated away" over the next two decades. That forecast may be a little off, but there's no question that virtually every industry is actively looking for better ways to manage traditional tasks and processes. If you build your career around the tasks that your company needs today, you may be in trouble if those tasks become obsolete. Again, you'll find the star performers don't get caught by surprise. They *lead* their companies into new ways of delivering results.

Moreover, becoming obsolete isn't a challenge you can safely ignore for a few decades. James Altucher, a successful entrepreneur and best-selling author, warns that a widespread "new paradigm" for American business is to replace full-time career employees with temp staffers and to outsource work whenever possible:

Most jobs that existed 20 years ago aren't needed now. Maybe they never were needed... I'm on the board of directors of a temp staffing company with one billion dollars in revenues. I can see it happening across every sector of the economy. Everyone is getting fired. Everyone is toilet paper now.

Finally, there's another, more subtle reason to focus your efforts on achieving results rather than just completing tasks: You'll be much happier.

Management consultant Patrick Lencioni says that one of the major reasons that employees feel literally miserable about their jobs is an absence of tangible, measurable results (a condition he calls "immeasurement"):

> Great employees don't want their success to depend on the subjective views or opinions of another human being. That's because this often forces them to engage in politics and posturing, which is distasteful for a variety of reasons, not the least of which is the loss of control over one's destiny. Employees who can measure their own progress or contribution are going to develop a greater sense of personal responsibility and satisfaction than those who cannot.

Former General Electric CEO Jack Welch echoes this point: "Over the past 12 years, I've spoken to more than 500,000 people around the world and I always ask audiences, 'How many of you know where you stand in your organization?'" he says. "Typically, no more than 10% raise their hands. That's criminal!"

CHAPTER 6

Results: Performance Metrics

"Everything that can be counted does not necessarily matter;
everything that matters cannot necessarily be counted."
— Albert Einstein

"Can you explain a little more about what a 'result' is?" asks a reader.
"I recently started a job as a research chemist at a pharmaceutical
company, so I guess my goal is simply to discover new molecules. Are
molecules a tangible result? Eventually, some of my discoveries may
become successful drugs that could make millions of dollars for the
company, but I don't have anything to do with that part of the
business."

Yes, molecules count. So do a lot of other **direct results** that
contribute to a company's overall success — for instance, contract
renewals, sales transactions, project deadlines. These direct
results connect to higher-level **corporate results** — profits, brand
identity, market share, and so forth. "The toe bone is connected
to the foot bone, the foot bone is connected to the heel bone..."
Well, you get the picture.

Often, the connection between your own direct results and the
company's ultimate corporate results is a long and winding
road. As a direct result of his job, our research chemist discovers
a new molecule... and then many years later, his company
brings to market a new drug that has an explosive impact on
company profits. Along the way, literally hundreds of people —
other scientists, clinical trial managers, patent attorneys,
marketers, financial modelers, sales reps — contribute their own
efforts toward commercializing the initial discovery. Each of
these successful outcomes helps bring about the final corporate
result.

A human skeleton has 206 separate bones that connect with each
other; a good-sized business can have a far more complex
network of direct and corporate results. As a new employee,
you're naturally going to focus on the direct results that your job
was created to produce. But you'll probably do a far better job if

you understand how your results help achieve top-level company goals.

To give you a sense of the variety of direct and corporate goals that you're likely to encounter, here's an overview of some of the many types of results that employees are expected to achieve. (This is another dense list that you might want to skip. It won't be on the final exam. Heck, there won't even be a final exam.)

Nine Categories of Business Results

....

Financial Results: For the most part, these are the results that begin with dollar signs. They include revenues, profits, costs, margins, assets, liabilities, liquidity, and (for public companies) market capitalization or share price. Financial results tend to be the most basic measures of company success and health, so they get lots of attention by top management. Financial terms also have specific technical definitions that you should understand. If you're fuzzy about the difference between revenues and profits, for instance, don't expect to be taken seriously by your boss or other higher-ups in the company.

....

Operating Results: Operating results deal mostly with how the business functions internally — sales transactions, production units, billable hours, leads, win-loss ratios, renewals, Web and store traffic, project completion status, call center metrics, new product development, response time, event registrations, on and on. Operating results are usually not measured in dollars and cents, but there's almost always a direct link between an operating result (such as "subscription renewals") and overall company revenues and profits.

....

Quality Results: Most companies pay close attention to at least a few quality measures, such as defects, reliability, performance, usability, and accuracy. In addition, reviews, ratings, and awards by outside organizations are often considered part of this category.

....

Customer Results: These are outcomes that are particularly important to sales and marketing employees. Customer results include such metrics as customer satisfaction, renewal rates, loyalty, market share, number of active customers, frequency of customer interaction, brand reputation, company visibility, influence, and trustworthiness. Much of this data is collected through surveys and interviews.

....

Innovation Results: Especially in technology and consumer markets, innovation is an especially critical result. Innovation can be tricky to measure, but a common standard is the percentage of company sales generated by new products or services.

....

Management Results: For the most part, management results reflect how well individual managers maximize the output of their teams. These results typically include revenue per employee, utilization rates, efficiency, employee retention, absenteeism, and skill or knowledge levels (typically measured in terms of credentials, training, published articles, or public presentations). People-intensive businesses, especially services, tend to track these results aggressively.

....

Social Results: This category usually reflects the personal values of a company's management. Social results may include financial support for religious, community, or arts groups, charitable and political donations, diversity goals, and perhaps even employment for family members. If you find yourself working for a company that emphasizes social goals, don't be surprised to find that top management will sometimes make "bad" business decisions in order to achieve higher-priority social results.

....

Internal Political Results: Within a company, managers and executives tend to compete with each other for resources and influence, both for themselves and for their teams. That's usually a healthy "survival of the fittest" process that rewards aggressive leadership and strong results. But internal politics can get out of control, and again you may find that managers make self-serving decisions that aren't in the best interest of their company.

....

Risk Mitigation Results: Risk mitigation is any outcome that reduces a company's exposure to risk, theft, financial instability, lawsuits, bad debts, or unexpected costs. These are tricky results to quantify, since the value becomes apparent only when some event *doesn't* happen. But reducing exposure to risk is nevertheless an important outcome; if a risk isn't prevented, the negative impact can sometimes be pretty serious.

....

This kind of complexity raises an obvious question: How do your new company's managers keep all these results properly aligned? How do they know when a single employee, a single department, or a single division is performing well (or not so well)?

The short answer: *Performance metrics.*

If you look at how individual managers track the results produced by Scott the programmer, Gertrude the event planner, or Hank the sales rep, you'll probably find that all of these employees get regular performance assessments that are based on their job functions.

In turn, their bosses also get performance assessments based on *their* job functions... all the way up the corporate hierarchy to the CEO, whose performance is assessed by the board of directors (or by the company's shareholders, who can signal their disapproval by dumping the company's stock).

It's no secret that this system of performance assessments is often flawed. But somehow on a company-wide scale, it usually works. Virtually every employee in your new company — including you — will probably get regular feedback on job performance, formal or informal. If a small link in the company's network of results gets broken, the performance assessment process tends to highlight the problem and make sure it's fixed. (Yes, your mileage may vary. But this is pretty much how well-run companies operate.)

"Okay," you say. "That sounds reasonable enough. I can live with constructive criticism."

Hold on a moment: There's more.

In most companies that are growing fast and trying to outperform their rivals — typical market leaders, in other words — performance assessments tend to create intense *internal competition.* The employees who score highest on their assessments are rewarded with promotions, bonuses, commissions, private offices, and fatter budgets. Employees who are just average or below average get few rewards and the less desirable assignments. Managers may even face some variation of the "up or out" career policy found in the armed forces and in tenure-track colleges: If you're not promoted within a defined period of time, you're gone.

That's a little more aggressive than "constructive criticism."

Of course, if you enjoy the challenge of competing against your peers, of constantly testing yourself, of winning the big prizes — none of this system of performance assessments will bother you. To use the inevitable sports metaphor, you know that keeping score is an essential part of the game.

But if you're *not* a competitive personality... well, you should probably take a closer look at what happens to employees in your new company who are just average performers. Companies that accept relatively modest levels of performance tend to be comfortable, secure places to work. But there are almost always important tradeoffs: lower overall pay, fewer merit-based promotions, and sometimes a negative company reputation that makes it hard to switch jobs later in your career.

And then there are all the companies somewhere in the middle. Here, you'll find fairly haphazard use of performance metrics — heavy reliance on subjective evaluations, dubious benchmarking methods, inconsistent follow-through on assessment results. Nobody understands or trusts the system, so your new colleagues will probably tell you the assessment process is unfair, insulting, and a waste of time. They're probably right.

How to Ace Your First Review

You probably won't get a formal performance review during your first hundred days, but it's still important to lay the groundwork for your future reviews. You want your boss to say "Keep up the good work!" instead of "I'm glad to see you're finally getting your act together."

A few guidelines:

✓ **First, identify the critical metrics:** It's human nature to cherry-pick the specific metrics where you excel. ("I don't answer many customer service calls, but my answers are always meticulously researched.") Find out what aspects of performance are currently top-of-mind with your boss, and make sure your numbers are excellent in these specific areas. Also, be sure you score reasonably well in *team-related* performance issues.

✓ **Avoid surprises:** Ask your boss for regular feedback on how you're doing. This is a reasonable request during your first hundred days; later on, constant requests for status reports may become annoying. Use discretion here.

✓ **Do something big:** Did you personally rescue a big account? Recruit the conference keynote speaker? Write the entry application that won a major industry award? These achievements won't show up in standard performance metrics, but be sure your boss knows the details during your assessment meeting.

✓ **Track your own results:** Try to collect personal data on important performance metrics in a notebook, preferably annotated with information that provides some context. ("Yes, I made fewer calls in October, but that's because I was doing product demos at three major trade shows.")

Even better, says financial advisor Mike Gonnerman, you can build your own "personal performance report" using basic spreadsheet tools. "Graph the weekly numbers for each of your major goals — sales, billable hours, calls handled, whatever," he says. "Add separate graphs for completion benchmarks on the projects you're working on. You'll have a really detailed, honest measure of your own progress." He adds: "This is probably too much to show to your boss, but it's great discipline for you as an individual."

✓ **Understand how your evaluations impact your job:** The perennial post-assessment question always seems to be "Do I get a raise?" Before you ask that potentially-awkward question, do basic research on how your company's performance assessments play a role in promotions, assignments, and compensation. Or you might want to ask for a reward that's more valuable *to you* than cash, such as a more flexible schedule, stock options, extra vacation time, extra overtime hours, a more impressive title, company-paid training, or even a better parking slot.

✓ **Get ahead of any negatives:** If you expect to hear about a performance problem ("Buffy, you can't keep driving stakes through the hearts of those vampires in accounting"), be ready to show that you're *already* taking remedial action. ("I know, boss. Last week I signed up for an anger management class.")

✓ **Keep your feelings under control:** When your boss confronts you with your real or imagined failings, the result is bound to be stressful. According to Tom Coens and Mary Jenkins, authors of *Abolishing Performance Appraisals*, "Too often, appraisal destroys human spirit and, in the span of a 30-minute meeting, can transform a vibrant, highly committed employee into a demoralized, indifferent wallflower who reads the want ads on the weekend." In fact, your boss probably hates the evaluation ritual as much as you do, and Coens and Jenkins point out that performance recommendations are often known to be "distorted and unreliable." In other words, don't take this unpopular experience too personally.

★

The Productivity Myth

While we're exploring types of results, we can't neglect the most famous of all employee metrics: "productivity." It probably won't take long for you to have this conversation with your new boss:

YOU: "So what are your expectations?"

BOSS: "Well, I'd like you to be as productive as possible. We pride ourselves here on being the most productive office in the company."

YOU: "Um, what exactly does that mean?"

BOSS: "You know, being productive. Getting a lot done. Preferably as quickly as possible."

YOU: "Gosh, thanks for this input. I'll do my best..."

To an economist, employee productivity is a simple concept: It's the average output, sometimes measured in revenue dollars, that a group of employees generates. For instance, "Our telesales reps bring in an average of $2,500 in orders per day." Or "Our proofreaders have a quota of five pages of technical text per hour."

An economist will also make the point that the group's output should consist of *measurable results,* typically for one specific task. When you mix up several tasks (especially time spent on administrative tasks like attending meetings and filling out expense reports), "productivity" metrics have little value for measuring an individual employee's work. "I spend two hours a day reading my email" is usually not a meaningful measure of productivity.

Wall Street analysts have an even narrower way to measure productivity: They simply divide a company's total annual revenues by the total company headcount at the end of the year. The result is a measure called "sales per employee." Sales per employee is essentially a tool for benchmarking how efficiently a company uses *all* of its employees — including managers and support people — to deliver goods and services to paying customers. Microsoft generates $678,383 in average sales per employee; a $1 million startup with ten employees generates only $66,667 per employee. That's a hard productivity gap to close.

Notice that productivity is essentially a *group* measurement. Imagine a sales superstar who brings in a million dollars a year in revenue—a pretty impressive example of productivity, no? But how good are his results if our superstar has five full-time helpers who generate leads, prepare proposals, set up demos, and schedule appointments? Chances are, the superstar's six-person team costs their company about $500,000 in salaries, commissions, and other overhead... half of the revenue they bring in. When you calculate productivity based on the results achieved by a whole team, the superstars often look far less impressive.

When most bosses talk about productivity, however, it's pretty clear that they're not talking like economists or Wall Street analysts. The boss's practical definition of productivity is usually something like "working hard," "putting in long hours," "always looking busy." Pay attention to how often your new boss uses language like this: If this is how he measures your results, don't expect a sophisticated appreciation of your accomplishments. Just look busy.

★

When Performance Metrics Go Wrong

Browse through our list of results and you'll notice that performance is sometimes hard to measure. Customer satisfaction, software usability, brand loyalty, risk avoidance— there's no question that these are real and important outcomes. But the measurement methods that companies use to track these outcomes tend to involve a lot of guesswork and subjectivity. As a rookie employee, there's rarely anything you can do to improve this situation. Nevertheless, watch out for badly-implemented metrics like these that may distort your personal accomplishments:

Unreliable satisfaction surveys: Customer surveys have become widely popular as a way to track employee performance, in large part because the data feels tangible and precise. In reality, much of the raw data comes from small, non-representative samples, the questions often don't address major customer concerns, and the results are highly variable depending on when and where the survey takes place. Moreover, employees often discover that it's easier to rig the data collection process than to actually deliver good results. (The most notorious example is the satisfaction surveys that auto service reps give to customers... along with a warning that any score less than perfect will mean that the mechanics will "lose their bonuses.")

Inputs vs. outputs: Whenever it's hard to quantify an indirect outcome like "innovation" or "brand recognition," companies tend to fall back on measures of how much they *spend* to achieve these outcomes. A company that spends all its R&D dollars patching up obsolete products isn't being innovative; a company that buys lots of ineffective ads isn't investing in brand recognition. Eventually, customers wander off in search of real results, and top management wonders what went wrong...

"Soft-dollar" forecasts: When companies invest in cost-cutting strategies, a common source of bad metrics is the use of so-called "soft dollars" in return-on-investment forecasts. Jeremy Eden and Terri Long, co-authors of a nifty collection of productivity tips called *Low-Hanging Fruit,* point out that corporate projects are often sold on the basis of cost savings that no one is actually responsible for delivering:

> A manager says to you, 'If we get the new software, our 100 operators will be able to save 30 minutes of manual reporting a day, which is worth $350,000!' You should then ask whether that person plans on reducing staff. If the manager says, 'No, we can't do that, but we will save a lot of time,' then you know you are dealing with soft dollars that will never hit the bottom line. Maybe buying the software is a good idea — but not because the purchase will save money.

Numbers without direction: If a metric behaves as if it's on auto-pilot, never creeping up or down, there's a good chance it's not measuring any kind of performance that employee efforts can influence. The same is true of numbers that may move up or down, but where the movement itself doesn't tell you anything actionable. For instance, if visitors spend 30 seconds more on your Web site, is that good (more interest in content) or not good (harder to find what they want)? If you can't make decisions based on how your performance metrics change, the numbers are probably a waste of everyone's time.

Black-box algorithms: Many so-called "Key Performance Indicators" (otherwise known as KPIs) start out as simple, clean numbers that most people can easily understand. But over time, managers often plug in other supposedly-important factors and weighting, turning the simple metric into a formula that almost no one understands. No surprise: An incomprehensible KPI usually has zero influence on anyone's performance.

CHAPTER 7

Results: Figuring Out What Matters

"When [scientists] discover the center of the universe,
a lot of people will be disappointed
to discover that they are not it."
– Bernard Bailey, comic book artist

"Okay, I get the idea that my job exists to produce results," says
another reader. "But how do I find out whether these results actually
matter to my company? I can't find any consensus."

This is a surprisingly common question. Almost certainly, you didn't hear an answer — an honest answer, that is — during the recruiting process. Your job description will never say that you're the corporate equivalent of cannon fodder. If you're lucky, a senior executive might greet new hires by saying, "You're all important members of our team. Our company is like a great chain… as strong as the weakest link." Yeah, right.

The truth is, some employees and some departments are more "strategic" than others. Moreover, some of the individual tasks you perform are far more important than others on your to-do list. Heck, while we're sharing ego-deflating news, here's another reality: Many companies and their products are unimportant to their customers. If your favorite brand of toothpaste vanished tomorrow, how much would you care?

Self-esteem is important, of course, so you'll probably find that your new company has a noble-sounding mission statement and your new boss will tell you a self-serving story about the impact of the department you just joined. "We proofread company publications," your boss might say. "If a typo ever appeared in our annual report, shareholders would immediately dump their stock and the company would go under."

Well, no. Ignore the self-esteem hot air and instead think about the importance of your results at four critical levels:

Your personal career — What accomplishments will look best on your resume and annual assessment? If you don't have a chance to hit home runs in your present job, can you make a move to another department that's more upwardly mobile?

Your boss — Your boss may do a fair amount of self-promotion — for instance, giving a speech to a trade association or serving on an impressive-sounding committee. These efforts may not produce much direct value to your new company, but bosses who *look* like winners tend to get more budget money and other resources for their department. So it's often in your interest to help out whenever you can.

Your department — As a newbie, you won't be given important assignments until you've proven yourself. But don't wait for lightning to strike: Identify important department tasks and ask your boss for a chance to show what you can do. If possible, become a problem solver. Show leadership potential. And stay away from projects that really don't matter to anyone.

Your company — You probably won't be in a position to impact corporate revenues, so look for out-of-the-ordinary ways to make the company look good. Impress an important stakeholder, find a big cost saving, or get written up (positively, of course) in the media. An obscure Nordstrom's shoe salesman once decided that it would be okay to sell a single shoe to a one-legged customer. That story has been told and retold literally thousands of times, and it's now become a defining symbol of the company's exceptional commitment to customer service.

In practical terms, think of your first hundred days as an extension of your job-hunting campaign. Your goal should be to identify the hottest career opportunities inside your new company and be ready to position yourself as a prime candidate for any new openings. (Just as important, you should also be ready to reject offers that won't help your career.) If the department you've just joined is already doing important work, you won't need to look further. However, if you've accidentally wandered into a corporate backwater, you should probably look for a better place to show off your talents.

How do you figure out where the important work is happening in your new company? Here are a few useful clues:

Clue #1: The incentive system: Companies typically pay bonuses to reward narrowly targeted results—for instance, revenue growth, high profits, employee productivity, better renewal rates, on-time completion of contracts or products, and similar goals. Incentives are an indication that the company is willing to lay out serious cash to achieve these results, so pay close attention to the plan's priorities even if you're not interested in playing the incentive game yourself.

Incentive plans also signal the relative importance of personal vs. team results. Personal incentives (for example, prizes for top sales rep of the month) usually reward individual initiative, while team incentives (such as profit sharing) reward results that reflect more collaborative efforts. This is an important signal: If the focus of most incentives is on team results, top management may have decided not to encourage individual superstars. Adjust your personal strategy accordingly.

Clue #2: The corporate budget: How a company spends its money is typically a reflection of top management priorities. A company that wants to grow sales puts money into its sales organization; a company that values innovation almost always funds a fat R&D budget. Ideally, you should get yourself assigned to a part of the company that is generously funded. That's where the business is expected to grow.

Clue #3: Revenue growth rates: Most companies operate with a portfolio of individual products and business units. Some are market leaders or cash cows; others may be stagnant or even in decline. Be very cautious about getting assigned to any segment of the company that's in trouble (a typical sign is a multi-year sales decline in excess of 10%). The standard corporate strategy for declining businesses is to "shoot the wounded"—that is, to sell or close down operations and lay off all the employees. You won't get much advance notice, so move quickly to line up a transfer or a new job.

Clue #4: Bragging rights and heroes: Notice the results that employees and company managers like to brag about. 3M employees are proud of being innovators, Zappos people think their order fulfillment is fantastic, Cisco showcases its "thought leaders." Clearly, these kinds of bragging rights say a lot about company priorities. Again, make sure you understand *why* these results are important to the company, and develop an understanding of how these results are achieved. You may not feel that warehouse operations are a fascinating subject, but if you work for an e-commerce company the people you want to impress are probably passionate about inventory management and fulfillment times. They'll be impressed if you know something about what makes their company special.

In addition, watch for *individual* heroes in your own department—the field service rep who flew cross-country over the weekend to fix a customer's order-entry system or the CFO who worked six straight weeks without a break to get a prospectus ready.

Clue #5: The path to the top: Check out the backgrounds of the company's top executives. You'll often find that companies recruit the majority of their senior people from a narrow range of lower-level jobs. Department stores and retail chains like to promote employees who have been successful as buyers; technology companies like leaders who have worked as programmers and product managers; media companies like executives who have worked as advertising sales reps (preferably selling to big accounts). Without these specific credentials, you won't have a history of producing the results that employers feel are vital for success in these industries.

Clue #6: What drives shareholder value: At the top of the corporate ladder, the results that matter most to C-level executives and board members are usually a metric called "shareholder value." For a public company, that's essentially the stock price; for a privately owned company or a venture startup, shareholder value ultimately represents the likely selling price of the business (even if there are no immediate plans to find a buyer). You should understand how different results impact the value of the business: For a low-revenue startup, for example, the most important results for investors are usually rapid revenue growth; for an older business, profits and market share tend to be more important.

Clue #7: High-profile failures: Finally, study the experience of employees who *didn't* succeed. For instance, managers with job experience in big companies usually expect to spend time developing elaborate business plans and infrastructure for new programs, but if they move to an entrepreneurial startup it's likely that their new bosses will expect immediate hands-on results... and when these results take too long, the new guy gets the axe.

How Money Matters

There's a common business rule that says, "The only results that matter are financial results. If something you're doing doesn't make money, it's a waste of time" (or words to that effect).

True? It depends on your perspective. Money is a pretty good yardstick for making decisions about where to invest company resources. For instance, should the marketing department spend $100,000 to launch a social media campaign or use those dollars to upgrade the company's packaging? In large part, the decision will depend on the expected return on each investment (ROI) — the additional profit that social media will bring in compared to the packaging upgrade. (Of course, both investment options may turn out to have lousy ROIs, so neither project may get funded.)

Thousands of individual survival-of-the-fittest decisions like this get made throughout any large company, and — at least in theory — the majority of the company's dollars end up invested in projects and segments that are likely to deliver the highest return. Money literally becomes the company's measure of importance. And as a new employee, following the money isn't a bad career strategy.

But there's another perspective that's also important. Money may help measure results, but it's not always a reliable goal to help *achieve* those results. A good example: A few years ago, Howard Schultz, the visionary CEO of the Starbucks coffee company, decided to step back from running daily operations. A group of financial guys took over managing the company, focusing their attention on making everything more efficient. They slashed costs, dumped menu items that weren't selling well, and standardized store layouts. Their strategy was to make the company more profitable, and thus boost the stock price.

Alas, their plan failed. What they forgot was that lots of competitors sell coffee (usually for much lower prices than Starbucks). Customers had been drawn to Starbucks for largely intangible reasons — the stores were fun, sometimes unpredictable, friendly, and definitely not boring. In their pursuit of efficiency, the financial managers committed the ultimate sin: Starbucks became boring. Customers went elsewhere for their coffee fixes, and the stock price plunged.

Howard Schultz eventually came back and launched a new round of innovative makeovers for the company's stores, menus, and loyalty programs. The customers also came back... and Wall Street once again fell in love with the company's stock. In the fickle world of consumer marketing, Schultz later explained, "The future of Starbucks is linked to our ability to create game-changing innovation." In other words, money is sometimes just a by-product of a less-tangible result.

Starbucks is not an unusual case, by the way. Almost every successful company owes its profitability and value to some largely-intangible factor. A mom-and-pop hardware store may do well because it occupies an ultra-convenient location, a mid-sized legal firm may have a friendly receptionist who remembers every client's name, a fast-growing technology startup may have one key programmer who is a master of exotic algorithms that no competitor can figure out. Like Howard Schultz's "game-changing innovation" at Starbucks, these intangibles should eventually contribute to better financial results. But if you're convinced that dollars and cents are the only *direct* measure of value, you'll always have a hard time understanding why some intangible factors are so important.

Hidden Agendas

Cynthia Shapiro, a former HR executive who reveals the "hidden agenda" of big-company politics in a book called

Corporate Confidential, makes the point that even well-run companies suffer from problems they really don't want to expose to outsiders. Occasionally, top management hopes to hide a major crisis or business vulnerability; more often, someone has just made a dumb mistake that annoys a few customers. The typical employee response, says Shapiro, is to ignore the situation and hope the problem will go away by itself. That's wrong, she argues: Pitching in when a major pain issue emerges demonstrates engagement and initiative, and may make a real contribution the company's public image and overall success:

> That [public image] is what gives the company stature in the marketplace, draws additional clients, and brings in more money. The more success and money a company has, the less likely they are to operate from a place of fear, doing things like panic layoffs and reorganizations. More money also means more rewards to valued employees. Companies who are successful in the marketplace are happier places to work. They have a joyous energy, offer increased opportunities, and new promotions.

It's unlikely that you'll have a chance to pull your new company back from a precipice in your first hundred days, of course. But Shapiro's point is that you can demonstrate loyalty and commitment in many small ways. If your new company is losing clients or has an employee morale problem, don't turn your back on the issue — get involved and try to be helpful. Be a cheerleader. Fix mistakes. Tell your boss you're enthusiastic about your job (and if that's not how you honestly feel, dig a little deeper to see if you can find a more positive side to your experience). Heck, pick up trash by the front walk. Do the little things you'd take care of by yourself if you were a responsible part-owner of the business.

"Companies love employees with passion," Shapiro says. "It is those employees that they want at the top."

CHAPTERS 8-10

Reputation

In a typical work environment, people rely on each other more than they usually do in a classroom or a small business. Establishing trust, responsibility, flexibility, and basic likability become important from the moment a new employee joins the team—and over time, an employee's reputation largely defines his or her relationship with the entire company. If that reputation is positive, attractive opportunities are likely to open up quickly. If it's not positive... the result is almost always a dead-end career.

The three chapters in this section offer advice on how to leverage first impressions, how to manage your ongoing reputation, and how to handle the specific challenge of a first-time management-level job.

CHAPTER 8
Reputation: First Impressions

"You never get a second chance to make
a great first impression."
—Olivia Fox Cabane

"Help! What should I wear on my first day at work? If I violate the company dress code or do something goofy, I'll never live it down!" Newly-hired employees tend to obsess about making a good first impression... and the truth is, they're right to worry. Research shows that human beings often make snap judgments about newcomers in the first *few seconds* of their acquaintance. That's even more brutal than three-minute dating.

Fortunately, many awkward first impressions can be turned around, in work as well as courtship. But it's better to start building your reputation with as few fumbles as possible.

In your first days on the new job, bear in mind that the people you most want to impress are not your Facebook buddies or the gang you hang out with on the weekends. For better or worse, you need to earn the respect and trust of managers, senior staff, and other veteran employees—mostly older and more conservative types. Author Charles Murray says the people who run large organizations are likely to be what he calls "curmudgeons"...

> ... highly successful people of both genders who are inwardly grumpy about many aspects of contemporary culture, make quick and pitiless judgments about your behavior in the workplace, and don't hesitate to act on those judgments in deciding who gets promoted and who gets fired.

Curmudgeons "don't want to sound like geezers," Murray adds. "So they never admit that they judge you on the basis of their inner curmudgeon—but they do. If you want to get ahead, you should avoid doing things that will make them write you off."

Fair warning.

We could assemble a long list of scenarios that might trigger negative first impressions. But then you'd never work up the courage to even show up for work. In reality, most employers are pretty forgiving about small gaffes—spilling coffee on the conference room carpet, forgetting your new boss's name, wandering in late for your first staff meeting—as long as you don't keep repeating these kinds of mistakes. More importantly, focus on a few BIG areas where making a strong first impression can immediately make a difference in how you're perceived:

In your first few days...

✓ **Be respectful toward everyone:** No rough language, no sexist behavior, no rudeness toward underlings, no yelling. You don't know who'll be upset, and it's distinctly possible that you'll be fired immediately. (Yes, this happens.)

✓ **Dress for success:** Unless you never, ever meet with customers, your new company will probably want you to wear "appropriate" or "professional" clothing. Companies typically see dress codes as part of their corporate branding, and they're especially sensitive about the appearance of any senior employees—for instance, lawyers and management consultants—who are going to work closely with high-level clients. Look carefully and you'll also notice that the quality of clothing often signals an employee's position in the corporate hierarchy. Worker bees wear blue jeans or uniforms; the CEO wears Armani suits. (If you're better dressed than your boss, however, watch out.)

✓ **No jokes:** Many people use humor to build rapport with new colleagues. It often has the reverse effect, says Fay Vincent, former CEO of Columbia pictures and an ex-commissioner of Major League Baseball: "Your sense of humor is easily misread as patronizing and clumsy," he warns. "If you still think that telling a joke or relating a humorous story is somehow important to making a point, run it past your spouse or a trusted friend first. Never joke about serious matters."

✓ **Radiate confidence:** "Right from the beginning, it's incredibly important to look like the company was lucky to get you," says Karen Schwartz, a New York school administrator. "There was a job I badly wanted in the admissions department of a private school, but when I showed up to apply I found there were already dozens of candidates waiting ahead of me, all looking ultra-professional. When I introduced myself to the lady in charge, I simply said, 'If you don't hire me, you'll be making a big, big mistake.' She told all the other applicants to go home and hired me on the spot."

When you start working on your first assignments...

✓ **Wildly exceed expectations:** As a newbie, you probably won't get high-profile assignments. But that shouldn't stop you from doing a truly extraordinary job on a routine task. Knock the ball out of the park by doing extra research, by beating your deadline, by working extra hours, by volunteering for unpleasant tasks. Your initiative will be noticed. "Superior performance is extremely rare, and it stands out," Charles Murray points out. "That statement applies to every job in the organization, no matter how junior."

✓ **Never blow off an assignment:** Lately, older managers have begun to complain that some of their younger employees simply ignore deadlines, typically without offering any excuse beyond "I was too busy." Your college instructors may have tolerated this behavior — and allegedly that's the main source of the problem — but being unreliable means you'll rarely get to work with more challenging projects or higher-value clients.

✓ **Polish your writing skills:** In a modern office, the written word — memos, reports, correspondence, proposals,

86

email—often puts you in front of more people than face-to-face encounters. If your writing is full of typos and misspellings, is disorganized or careless... you're in trouble. Find a literate friend who will proofread *everything* you write, and invest serious time in learning spelling, punctuation, and good sentence structure. Of course, if you already write well, you might ask your boss if you can help out with blog posts, newsletters, sales letters, reports, and all the rest of the writing backlog that's probably choking your boss's inbox.

When you start meeting your new co-workers...

✓ **Watch the clock:** There's no such thing as "fashionably late" in the corporate world. The assumption is that *everyone* has a busy schedule, so a junior employee who shows up five minutes late has stolen time from everyone in the room. The one exception: like politicians, high-ranking bosses often show up late as a way of demonstrating their own enormous importance. Wait thirty years before you try this approach yourself.

✓ **Work the house:** Experienced public speakers try to show up early and spend time getting to know people in their audience. The same approach works well with staff meetings, client presentations, and even social events. Do some background checking on people you're likely to meet, and then spend time chatting with early-bird attendees (and try to remember their names). By the time the rest of the crowd arrives, you'll know a good deal about the audience's hot buttons—and you'll look like you're already an insider with lots of friends in the room.

✓ **Be discreet:** Your co-workers don't want to hear about your medical problems, your love life (or lack thereof), your politics, the raw deal you got at your last job, your eccentric relatives, your enormous salary, or the cool characters on your bowling team. If you're a compulsive chatterbox, leave your co-workers in peace and hire a therapist for $300 an hour. Everyone will be happier.

✓ **Don't cheat:** Your colleagues may tell you it's okay to fudge your expense account or call in sick when you want a day off. They may encourage you to tweak research results, hide complaint letters, or overcharge a client. If your boss catches you doing anything like this—and he probably will—you'll almost certainly be marked as an employee who can't be trusted.

Competence vs. Chemistry

"I'm an expert in tax law, and my new job includes attending social events to get prospective clients interested in our services," a reader says. "How can I possibly communicate a meaningful message about my technical competence in just a few seconds?"

With all due respect, you're probably asking the wrong question. Yes, it's important to tell your prospects what you do for a living—"I'm a tax attorney at Dewey Cheatham & Howe." But don't invest any of your precious first-impression seconds in convincing your prospect that you're an especially *good* tax expert. If you claim to be a tax expert—or a plumber, or a travel agent—most of us will take your basic competence at face value. Save the details for a follow-up meeting.

> **Instead, focus on great *personal chemistry*.** Be likable, enthusiastic, engaging. Smile, look the other person in the eye, listen closely to what they're saying... well, you know the drill. This is the message your prospects want to hear, and you can communicate it quite clearly with a combination of body language and well-chosen words.

A good deal of research underscores the key role of personal chemistry. For instance, here's how clients ranked the importance of eight qualities in a professional services provider:

1. **Competence**
2. **Credibility**
3. **Trustworthiness**
4. **Likability**

5. **Business savvy**
6. **Responsiveness**
7. **Empathy**
8. **Communication**

Naturally, competence and credibility come first in a professional relationship. But notice that almost all the other items on this list are *relationship* qualities. Even if you manage to persuade your prospect that you're a technical superstar, you probably won't inspire confidence and interest unless you also create an aura of likability, trust, empathy, and general niceness. (Show this list to anyone who regularly interacts with customers and clients and the answer will be, "So what else is new?")

Moreover, good personal chemistry usually enhances our sense of a person's competence and credibility. A recent study at the University of Massachusetts found that recommendations by a "likable" speaker tended to win over audience members even when the listeners disagreed with the speaker's advice and the evidence was weak. Apparently, most of us are suckers for a smile.

In case you need to brush up on your first-impression likability skills, here are a few tips from Michelle Lederman, a world-class advisor on personal chemistry and author of *The 11 Laws of Likability*:

On body language: "People are largely unaware of their natural body language," says Lederman. "The first time I was videotaped for a practice interview, my finger was winding and unwinding a lock of hair—not exactly the professional image I wanted to project."

> Even a few minutes of video recorded on a smartphone will show you what you need to know. Are you smiley but slouchy? Alert but offputtingly stern? Do you laugh nervously? Jingle something in your pocket? Even being marginally more conscious of the unspoken signals you are sending goes a long way, compelling you to stand straighter and maintain eye contact.

On being your authentic self: The "keystone to likability," says Lederman, is "to be your true self" when you meet new people. "We all know it when we're not being our natural selves. We feel uncomfortable, awkward even, perhaps unconfident and stressed." These inner feelings translate into visible behavior — tense, boastful, insincere — that many people find unpleasant. "When you show your authentic self, people will respond in kind, laying the bedrock for mutual understanding, connections, and growth."

On being an introvert: "Introverts are often naturally equipped to initiate connections because they tend to be good listeners. Don't try to emulate your wildly gregarious colleagues. Instead, pay attention to what makes *you* comfortable," says Lederman. "When you are part of a group conversation, do you prefer to listen to others and only speak up when you have something to say? Then by all means, do just that."

On the value of curiosity: "When you don't know how to start a conversation, start by being curious," says Lederman. "People love to talk — you just need to know how to get them going. Once you are talking, one subject can flow into the next one, which can flow into the next, and before you know it you've formed a connection."

Your LinkedIn Bio

As a job hunter, you probably set up a personal profile on LinkedIn. Now that you're collecting a paycheck, don't abandon LinkedIn — it's often your best shot at making a strong first impression with your new work contacts. William Arruda of Reach Personal Branding points out that the people you meet now routinely check your background online when they first meet you:

> Your colleagues are Googling you, potential clients, potential hiring managers — all the people who are making decisions about you are making those decisions based on your digital profile. And chances are, your LinkedIn profile is going to show up in the top three Google search results, often in the first spot. Even if people start searching with Google, they'll probably end up at LinkedIn.

However, it's likely that the profile you created for job searching needs a comprehensive rewrite, says Arruda. Instead of emphasizing a dry listing of skills and work history, your new profile should create an "emotional response" in the reader. The profile should define your "quirks and passions, your super-powers, your unique promise of value, the things that set you apart." Some specifics:

✓ **Get a professional photo:** "Selfies don't work," says Arruda. "It's absolutely critical to have an amazingly good head shot, so people can connect the person with the face." Since LinkedIn photos are relatively small, he adds, your face should fill up about 80% of the available image area, and the pose should show you either looking face forward or facing into the text area.

✓ **Tell a story:** A good way to create interest and engagement, says Arruda, is to cast your profile as a personal narrative. "Start with a bang to get the reader interested in reading further, and set the scene. I remember a social media analyst's profile that started with this sentence: 'When I was little, I wanted to be the next Barbara Walters.'"

✓ **Try writing in the first person:** It's much more engaging to talk about yourself as you would in a person-to-person conversation, say Arruda. "But this is an individual choice: Some people feel that first-person writing sounds like bragging and they start to water down their accomplishments."

✓ **Get other people to brag for you:** Your profile is an ideal place to mention awards, academic honors, advanced degrees, and endorsements, says Arruda. "This is a way to validate your personal brand without making claims yourself."

✓ **Include video and other media:** LinkedIn supports videos, photos, documents, and slideshows, Arruda points out. These elements "will differentiate your profile from your peers," he says. "And Google owns YouTube, so 65% of *video* search results end up on page one of Google search displays."

✓ **Test your revised profile on people who know you:** The critical question, says Arruda, is whether the profile genuinely reflects who you are. Ask your friends, trusted colleagues, mentors, and coaches if your profile inspires them to read further and discover more about you.

★

Asking for Help

When you're a newly-hired rookie, the last thing you want to ask is a dumb question. After all, you were supposedly hired to *be smart*. And now you're asking how to price a change order? You can just imagine the scornful laughter...

Except that's not what will happen, at least according to a team of Harvard Business School researchers who studied the social interactions that occur when people ask for advice. The surprising outcome, according to Alison Wood Brooks and Francesca Gino, is that advice-seekers are generally perceived as "*more* competent than those who do not seek advice."

Moreover, the respect you get from asking for advice actually increases when you ask an expert a relatively complex question. In effect, Brooks and Gino say, asking someone for advice is a form of flattery — a way of affirming the expert's "positive self-view."

But be careful about asking the wrong expert, Brooks and Gino warn. Asking an overly simple question can backfire, they say, because "the advisor may perceive that the advice seeker lacks the competence to complete an easy task." Even worse, asking experts about topics that are "unambiguously" outside their area of knowledge will probably "make the advice seeker seem less competent than not seeking advice at all or seeking advice from someone else."

In short, smart questions make you look smart, dumb questions make you look not-so-smart.

CHAPTER 9

Reputation: Building Your Brand

*"If a tree falls in the woods and no one is around to hear it,
does it still make a sound?"*

Shocking news! Most of the decision-makers in your new company — senior staff, executives, perhaps even your own boss — won't be closely watching you or other new recruits. Unless you're a "strategic" hire (usually a C-level or vice-presidential executive), your day-to-day accomplishments will go largely unnoticed. At this point in your career, you're simply not that important.

And that's a problem. Says career strategist Donald Asher: "The world is full of outstanding performers stuck in go-nowhere jobs, working for semiconscious bosses who don't appreciate what they've got and have no plans to reward star performers. Why? Sometimes because they don't even know they have a star performer working for them."

This isn't an impossible challenge to overcome, provided you're willing to do a little self-promotion. But many people would rather walk over burning coals. "The idea of bragging about myself makes me squirm," they say. "My accomplishments should speak for themselves."

The trouble is, your accomplishments usually don't speak all that clearly for you. You become "the guy who lifts weights" or "the new researcher who got tipsy at the company party." Or perhaps "the know-it-all from Silicon Valley." If you don't *manage* your reputation, your reputation is likely to drift into pretty random territory.

Moreover, managing a reputation is quite different from the kind of narcissistic chest-beating that most of us find painfully obnoxious. For the most part, your co-workers are going to be chiefly interested in how you'll interact with them as a new colleague and team member. They'll talk about your personal conduct, your relationships with other employees, and your specific on-the-job talents. Can they trust you? Will you carry your own weight? Are you smart? If your emerging reputation tells this story accurately, you're more likely to get credit for your work and accomplishments... and you'll probably get noticed more quickly as one of the company's rising stars.

How do you lay the groundwork for a great reputation? There are two basic steps:

First, Craft the Message

When the people in your company talk about you, you'd like them to say good things. But you also want them to remember what marketers call your "unique selling proposition" or your "brand promise" — a few words that define your special value to the company. "Clarissa is the only sales rep who's fluent in Spanish," "Hank is a dynamite C++ programmer," "Leona is the best tax lawyer we've ever hired." This kind of message sets you apart from most other employees and — ideally — puts you at the head of the line for assignments that will let you further show off your special talents and emphasize the results you're going to deliver.

Unlike a professional marketer, however, you can't just turn your selling proposition into an catchy advertising slogan. The words have to emerge spontaneously in conversation and survive the pass-along process more or less intact. That's a tough challenge.

That's why the second step of your unique selling proposition is a quality called *relevance*:

Second, Make Your Message Relevant

Clarissa may be proud of her ability to speak Spanish, but no one in her new company will give a hoot if the company has no Spanish-speaking customers. Somehow, she needs to *make her skill seem important to the success of the company*. For instance, she might do some informal market research into business opportunities in Latin America. She could network with experts, academics, and marketers in non-competing companies who know how to succeed in Spanish-speaking countries. And then

Clarissa could present an informal proposal about expanding the company's business into a major new market.

Whether or not Clarissa's proposal gets immediate action almost doesn't matter. She is now well positioned as the company's resident expert on Latin American expansion opportunities. She's not just a sales rep with a minor skill: She now stands out as a valuable market development resource. If her new company does decide to launch a marketing initiative in Latin America, Clarissa almost certainly will be invited to play a key role.

"Sounds like a lot of work," you might say. Well, yes. Building a reputation doesn't happen by itself. You need to give people a reason to talk about you. You need to volunteer to *do* things that will make you more important and interesting to the people you work with. You also need to focus your efforts on building a specific reputation—which often means passing up other attractive opportunities. In building her reputation as a Latin American expert, Clarissa may have to turn down an assignment to the fast-growing healthcare market. It's usually tough to build a focused reputation and be a generalist at the same time.

Building a Reputation in a Small Organization

"I've started working in a pretty small company (about 25 employees) where we all do more or less the same kind of projects. I can see it's going to be hard to stand out or build any kind of reputation. Suggestions?"

Small organizations present the classic challenge of how to become a "big frog in a small pond." It's easy to become visible when you work closely with just a few dozen people. But the scope of your reputation is also inherently limited.

A good way to stand out is to leverage a talent that you already possess, and to look for ways to make this talent useful to the rest of the people in your group. Some examples:

....

The Futurist: People in small organizations often feel like they need to catch up on recent trends—social media, e-commerce, mobile computing, email marketing, and the like. In these areas, they also implicitly trust the advice of new, young employees who are presumed to have special insights into this baffling new world.

....

The Number Cruncher: If you have any competence in math or statistics, you're in a good position to interpret survey data, performance metrics, and pricing decisions.

....

The Tech Guru: Every office needs a troubleshooter who knows the advanced features of the company's software and can fix misbehaving computers, printers, and network devices.

....

The New Projects Specialist: This is a good role for employees who are quick learners and like the challenges of breaking in new clients or managing pilot programs.

....

The Webmaster: It's hard to find an organization these days that doesn't have a Web site or at least a Facebook page. These sites inevitably need small updates and corrections, often on short notice. If you have basic HTML skills, you'll quickly become the company's go-to person for Web maintenance (and perhaps for more advanced online projects).

....

The Copywriter: If you can write effective promotional copy, you'll become a critical resource for anyone who needs help with a sales letter, Web copy, presentation scripts, or a major proposal. If your work generates positive results, you'll get credit as a rainmaker.

....

The Event Organizer: Even a small customer meeting typically involves fairly complex logistics, and an employee who does a good job here becomes highly visible.

....

★

Leveraging the Voice of the Customer

Salespeople have long enjoyed a near-monopoly as authorities on how customers think—and they're not shy about using that reputation to win arguments (or budget dollars). "If we raise prices by 3%, our biggest customers say they'll take a walk."

"Customers demand free shipping." "My contact at MegaWare says our tech support people take too long to answer the phone."

It's tough to argue with people whose friends write the big checks.

But salespeople aren't the only employees who can become customer experts. In fact, almost every major department in a modern company interacts with people on the customer side — providing post-sale services, developing products, collecting payments, conducting research, creating marketing materials, and so forth. And there's a good chance those customer folks have strong ideas about how to make their piece of the process work much better.

If only somebody would listen.

"We do listen," your new colleagues will complain. "Why, we sent out a satisfaction survey last month. And there's a Contact Us page on our Web site. We have an online forum for tech support questions. And our dealers can get in touch with the repair depot if a customer has a big problem. We're great listeners!"

This kind of thinking is probably the chief reason why there aren't many people in companies — other than salespeople — who have a reputation as authorities on what customers are thinking. If you're looking for a way to grow your reputation, becoming the "voice of the customer" is usually a wide open opportunity.

Here's how to develop your reputation for customer expertise:

✓ **Build one-on-one relationships:** This is crucial. Surveys and focus groups may help reveal fine distinctions in the world as you now see it, but they do a lousy job of discovering new out-of-the-box insights. You need to assemble a circle of colleagues and friends who'll tell you the honest truth... who'll spend time thinking about the issues you've raised over lunch, and who will then call you back the next morning with a brilliant suggestion.

✓ **Start with simple research interviews:** As a new employee, you probably won't talk with many customers or clients. But you're likely to have a few outside contacts you work with as part of your regular job—vendors, consultants, trainers, delivery services, and the like. Pick up the phone and start calling these people. Ask if you can have a few minutes for feedback on how to improve a small, tangible part of your relationship that they deal with—invoices, deliveries, perhaps your company's Web site. If they can't think of anything, ask which of their other vendors does a really outstanding job. Take notes, thank them for their advice, and follow up with a short thank-you note. Repeat a few dozen times, and start to cultivate the people who are most helpful.

✓ **Learn to drill down to pain issues:** Interviewing a customer is a bit like courtship: You start with safe topics, and as you build trust you gradually move into greater personal revelations. Your goal is to learn each customer's most pressing "pain issues"—the concerns that literally keep your interview subject awake at night. Helping customers solve pain issues builds passionately loyal fans, so whatever you learn can make you an especially valuable customer expert.

✓ **Become a spider on the wall:** If your company has an online forum, spend a few minutes every day reading the latest postings. Look for non-technical problem areas, unresolved grievances, and other evidence of how customers feel about your company. (If you have time, check out the competition as well.) Identify high-profile influencers and ask them for their feedback and advice.

✓ **Hang out at customer events:** You can probably skip conferences and trade shows where the attendees are people like you. But do spend time at events where your *customers* come to learn about new stuff. Listen to the chatter, collect business cards, and make follow-up calls when you get back to your office.

✓ **Leave the slide deck at home:** When you talk with a new contact, your objective is to listen for fresh thinking. That means no canned presentations, no sales pitches, no attempts to "validate" your own notions. If you feel awkward about having an unscripted conversation, just keep practicing. You'll get much better.

Doomed Projects and Clients from Hell

If you've ever watched the Food Network's *Restaurant: Impossible* show on TV, you've seen veteran chef Robert Irvine turn around failing restaurants and dramatically change the leadership styles of their owners. In each episode, Irvine works his tough-love magic with just two days of probing questions and a stream of drill-sergeant orders. His track record is stellar: Over 90% of the restaurants featured on the show are now "doing gangbusters," he claims.

Wouldn't it be fun to be a guy like this?

Then your new boss drops in to ask you about a possible new assignment. "We have a project that's in trouble," he says. "The client is going nuts and my own boss is worried. If you could help out, this would be a really great way to get visibility here."

Your boss may mean well, but if you value your reputation — run like a rabbit.

Unlike reality TV, corporate turnaround problems are almost always deeply messy. The solution may be obvious, but there are likely to be dozens of senior people whose own reputations will be at risk if the problem is solved in the "wrong" way. From a top management point of view, the least disruptive way to deal with a "client from hell" or a mismanaged project is usually to find a low-level scapegoat and take a hefty financial hit. There's rarely a role for a would-be turnaround hero.

Worse, it's dangerous for your reputation even to be associated with bad outcomes. "Wasn't Cindy involved somehow in that huge lawsuit we lost two years ago? I don't remember if it was her fault, but you better keep an eye on whatever she's doing…"

Here's how career guru Don Asher describes the drawbacks of working for a business unit that's in trouble:

> It used to be that it wasn't a bad thing to be in the worst business unit in an organization. The theory was that it would be easier to make a noticeable difference. The problem is that companies today rather ruthlessly cut off failing business units, so asking for a tough assignment may be step one in getting you fired, even if you are, relatively, successful. More important, by going to the worst business unit you are robbing yourself of a chance to work closely with the best people. Talent sharpens talent. There's nothing more insufferable than a truly talented person who has been living in isolation, without the challenge and balance of other talented people.

Asher also points out that there are certain "thankless tasks" that it's wise to avoid, if you can:

> A mechanical engineer told me he started out as a quality-control engineer until he realized it was the worst kind of assignment. 'If things are going well,' he told me, 'someone else will get the credit. When things start to go bad, you are responsible for sounding the alarm and correcting the problems. So you are always associated with the foul-ups, and rarely with a feel-good success story.'

Of course, as a new employee you probably won't have a choice of assignments. If there's any hint that a client or project might end up on the rocks, take these steps:

 Do your homework: Find out if your new client has a history of litigation against vendors, or if the executive in charge of your internal project is a well-known screw-up. If you spot a pattern, document everything you do — progress reports, email exchanges, meeting summaries, change orders.

✔ **Read the contracts:** Pay close attention to penalty clauses and deadlines (which are sometimes defined in a separate "service-level agreement"). If you end up in court—and this does happen—the specific contract language will carry vastly more weight than your feelings about what's "fair" or "reasonable."

✔ **Keep an eye on cash flow:** If possible, ask your finance department to let you know if a scheduled payment is late. That's often a sign that the relationship is falling apart.

✔ **Be careful about sharing your concerns:** Especially with internal projects, you may get tagged as a troublemaker if you ask someone in the corporate hierarchy for advice about handling an incompetent project manager. Remember that there is no such thing as boss/employee confidentiality. And *never* tell anything that you'd like to keep secret to an HR manager. Says Cynthia Shapiro of *Corporate Confidential*:

> The HR/personnel department is not allowed to be on your side, so don't give them any reason to suspect that you may become an inconvenience, problem, or liability of any kind. Treat HR as if you were speaking directly to the CEO, because you might as well be.

CHAPTER 10

Reputation: Looking Like a Leader

"Lose money for the firm, and I will be understanding.
Lose a shred of reputation for the firm, and I will be ruthless."
— Warren Buffett

Imagine you're about to meet the Queen of England.

You're nervous, perhaps even (let's be honest) terrified. You're afraid you'll do something wrong, something that insults the entire British Empire. Your friends will laugh at you. Your family... well, don't even think about next Thanksgiving.

But realistically, why are you nervous? By all accounts, the Queen is a very nice lady. She loves dogs. She has friends who gossip too much, just like the rest of us. And it's quite safe to insult the British Empire. The last time we got into a heavy argument with the Brits, you'll recall, we won. If the Queen frowns at you, just whisper "1776" in her royal ear.

Of course, your nervousness has nothing to do with reality. The fact is, almost everyone is a little awed by "leaders" — executives of big companies, powerful politicians, celebrities, senior military officers, billionaires, and other big shots. We feel like we're in the presence of people who are entitled to give orders.

But notice that we usually feel this sense of awe *before* we even meet these supposedly illustrious leaders face to face. We're not won over by the Queen's charisma or the CEO's bone-crushing handshake. Rather, we *expect* to be impressed... and then we respond right on cue.

One of the great secrets of leadership can be summed up in a few words: "Your reputation precedes you."

Meanwhile, the opposite secret is equally true: If you show up with no reputation at all, you probably won't inspire automatic respect. You'll have to *earn* your authority as a leader. Your decisions will be challenged, your shortcomings will be widely discussed.

How much does a leadership reputation matter? Not at all, if you're starting an entry-level job, because your authority over anything will be close to non-existent. At best, your boss might decide you're "management material" and recommend you for fast-tracking promotions. But that still leaves a long path to a significant leadership role.

However, if you're moving into your first management-level job, the job may come with much more authority and responsibility than you used to have—and that's where your leadership reputation typically becomes a sensitive issue. Suddenly, you're expected to be a stronger, more visionary leader. It's also likely you'll be in charge of a new team, in a new branch of the business where you have far less expertise than in your old job.

Moreover, failure at this point in your career can have a long-term career impact. Here's how Michael Watkins, a top expert on leadership transitions, sums up the importance of the impression you make when you take over a high-visibility leadership role:

> When leaders derail, their problems can almost always be traced to vicious cycles that developed in the first few months on the job. And for every leader who fails outright, there are many others who survive but do not realize their full potential. As a result, they lose opportunities to advance their careers and help their organizations thrive...
>
> Transitions are also periods of acute vulnerability, because you lack established working relationships and a detailed understanding of your new role. You're managing under a microscope, subject to a high degree of scrutiny as people around you strive to figure out who you are and what you represent as a leader. Opinions of your effectiveness begin to form surprisingly quickly, and, once formed, they're very hard to change.

Building a Leadership Reputation

Lucy, who was everyone's buddy when she ran the call center, has just been named the director of professional services. Her new staff members are a bunch of sharks who know her reputation... and they're not impressed. Will Lucy survive?

Lots of good, competent managers never quite succeed at developing a convincing "leadership reputation." If your business card says you're the boss, that's usually good enough for routine administrative tasks. You're unlikely to get pushback from your new staff if you spend most of your time "rearranging the deck chairs" instead of steering the ship.

But the real job of a leader is to make changes happen... to make the team more effective, to prune away obsolete tasks, to boost results. Inevitably, these changes will feel threatening to at least some of your employees — and they're going to launch a guerrilla campaign to raise doubts about what you're doing. That's when your leadership reputation becomes an essential asset.

Here are some specific tactics for your first hundred days:

In your first week or two on the job:

✓ **First, tell your own boss what you plan to do:** Get explicit permission to move quickly and decisively. If your boss steps in to reverse a decision you've just made, your reputation will be dead in the water.

✓ **Emphasize your service-enhancement plans:** Cynthia Shapiro, a savvy observer of behind-the-scenes corporate politics, points out that you'll get more support from your boss and other department heads if you focus on how you'll make *their* lives easier. "If you first offer yourself in service to all of them," she says, "you will put everyone at ease, opening the floodgates to inspire them to provide excellent service to you."

✓ **Define your own role:** Yes, you're ultimately responsible for everything that your department does. But that's not the same as *doing* everything yourself. In fact, trying to do everything leads directly to micromanagement and burnout. Instead, start by identifying the tasks that have the highest impact and that you're especially skilled at accomplishing. Delegate everything else to your team.

✓ **Immediately make a popular decision:** Before you start your new job, find at least one fairly obvious decision that your predecessor never got around to implementing — and make it happen right away. Try to solve simple problems that most of your staff think are no-brainers: a pending outsourcing contract, a server upgrade, a price increase, a failed project. Avoid (at least for now) complex technical issues that could go badly wrong.

✓ **Fire a troublemaker:** As quickly as possible, identify one or two employees who are widely regarded as jerks, deadwood, or chronic malingerers. Haul them into your office and fire them on the spot. (Check with the HR department first to make sure you don't leave the company open to a wrongful termination lawsuit.)

✓ **Review your team's performance metrics:** You're going to have lots of discussions about individual and group performance, so make sure you have all the facts. In particular, review competitive benchmarking data and employee assessments. If turnover is high, find out why people are leaving.

Start building strong relationships...

✓ **Get an outside perspective:** Talk to customers, vendors, consultants, and others who interact with your department. Look for specific areas where your operations have fallen behind the competition. If Amazon can ship orders daily, why is your delivery time so much slower? Have other firms eliminated annoying fees that you still charge? Are your sales contracts overloaded with unnecessary legalese? If you find friends outside the company who offer honest advice, arrange to meet regularly with them one-on-one.

✓ **Create an inner circle:** Leaders need friends to kick around ideas, but it's always risky to share your doubts and state secrets with the people who work for you. Find smart people who are outside your regular chain of command — perhaps a consultant, a financial expert, a recruiter, or a lawyer.

✓ **Develop alliances with your peers:** This gets tricky, because you may be competing with fellow managers for resources and influence. But arrange to have occasional lunches or an after-hours drink. Ask for advice and offer to team up on mutual problems.

✓ **Recruit your own talent scouts:** Invite selected friends, your inner circle, and your peers to act as informal talent scouts for your department. Explain that you're looking for exceptional people even though you don't have any immediate openings. You're always going to have turnover at unpredictable times, so make sure you can pick up the phone and invite a few highly-recommended candidates to meet with you as soon as openings occur.

Get your team behind you…

✓ **Interview all your direct reports:** As soon as possible, spend at least an hour with each of your direct reports and other key team members. Ask for their insights about whatever problem you've identified as a top priority… and ask what they recommend as a solution. You'll learn a lot about the problem — and more about their individual problem-solving abilities. You'll also make it clear that you want the whole team on board with *fixing* high priority problems. Nobody gets to sit on the sidelines.

✓ **Focus on your top performers:** It may be tempting to devote extra coaching time to your weakest staff members, but you'll usually get the best overall results by clearing away obstacles that make your best people less effective. Almost certainly, your top performers will quickly become part of your fan club.

✓ **Write thank-you notes:** One of the most powerful motivational tools in your manager's toolkit is a simple thank-you note. Send a note (not just an email) whenever one of your team members or extended network helpers does something really valuable. "Saying thank you all the time is a discipline," says best-selling business writer Suzy Welch:

> It's a practice, and a personality trait. It's a heart thing. Do it in your off hours, and chances are, you'll keep it going when you walk into the office. The upshot? A reputation as someone who understands that nothing good ever happens alone. Or put another way, the reputation of a natural leader.

✓ **Show the flag:** Leaders need to be seen, and that's hard to accomplish when you spend your day cooped up in your office or in meeting rooms. Instead, set aside time to just walk around and drop in on random employees. Ask how they're doing, and look for suggestions. Twitter CEO Dick Costolo is a fan of show-the-flag management; he takes regular afternoon walks around Twitter's offices and listens for unfiltered, on-the-ground information. "People are less likely to try to snow me in meetings," he told Inc. Magazine recently, "because they know I'm generally up to speed."

✓ **Set high standards for presentations and reports:** Start rejecting sloppy work — hard-to-read slides, badly-written emails and documents, incomprehensible statistical reports. Some managers try to find at least one error or faulty conclusion in every presentation they see (Microsoft's Bill Gates was a master of this tactic). It's a sneaky trick, but remarkably effective at convincing employees that they should strive for perfection.

✓ **Never undermine your own authority:** Leaders always take full responsibility for their decisions. Don't apologize for bad news. Don't blame a higher authority (the notorious "company policy"), your predecessor, or the terrible economy. Don't "share the pain" of people who have performed poorly or failed to follow your instructions.

★

The Vision Thing

Leaders often use a "big vision" as a way to communicate their plans for the future, and in fact a clear vision statement is a powerful tool for setting new priorities and emphasizing that business-as-usual is about to change. You're going to make literally dozens of major decisions during your first hundred days as a manager, some of which will no doubt freak out your employees. Showing how everything rolls up into a coherent strategy builds trust and confidence: "I guess this new guy has a plan."

But it's also possible to fumble a big vision.

Economics blogger Megan McArdle, who has reported on a good many failed government and corporate visions, says she sees common mistakes whenever "a brash new outsider is brought in to make over a government agency or turn around a company":

> Occasionally, folks in these roles think their job is just to come up with top-notch orders to give to their subordinates, and maybe have some meetings with key 'constituents' like politicians or board members or customers. What happens next is generally a spectacular crash and burn, because they alienate the folks they need on board to make their new program work. A smart leader knows that big strategic thinking and giving orders are the smallest parts of her job. The biggest is persuading people who are not invested in her agenda to carry out her grand plans — and, equally important, figuring out which plans to abandon because they can never get enough support to work.

How do you keep your vision from crashing and burning? Some tips:

✓ **First, align your plan with corporate goals:** This seems like common sense, but it's easy to focus too much on what your own team needs—and forget that the rest of the company might want different results or less investment in your own operations. If your company is about to announce layoffs, for instance, you probably won't get a green light for a strategy that calls for expanded staffing. Cynthia Shapiro points out that the time you spend asking other department heads about their needs will also show you "how your team fits in with other departments and the overall workings of the company."

> The ability to overlay the big-picture view onto your projects will make your team's efforts seem larger than life. Rather than simply producing within your area, with every project you will be improving systems and production for the company as a whole. And *that* is high-level leadership material.

✓ **Map out the implementation details:** Budgets, staff reassignments, pricing, new costs—you can't be vague about these things, and you can't simply delegate the details to a junior staffer. If something goes wrong—and it will, naturally—you own it.

✓ **Practice your pitch:** Try out your "vision" story with friends and colleagues until it's clear and compelling. If you're drawing on concepts that a well-known author has explored in print (for instance, on "disruptive technology" or "great customer service") buy copies in bulk and distribute them to your team and other stakeholders.

✓ **Be prepared for a serious selling effort:** It may take years to implement the changes you're proposing. Often, leaders just give up and quietly revert to the status quo. But if you succeed, top management will certainly notice that you've accomplished something pretty impressive.

CHAPTER 11

Satisfaction

In addition to the Three R's — Relationships, Results, and Reputation — there's a special success factor that neophyte employees too often overlook: *job satisfaction*. Landing a good job can be hard, so why rock the boat by asking if you actually *like* what you're doing?

And yet, the question of satisfaction is profoundly important as an ingredient in your long-term success. You're especially vulnerable at this point in your career — short on experience with real-world companies, short on choices, and short on self-knowledge about your personal goals. You'll get smarter as time goes by, but right now it's probably not wise to lock yourself into a life-long career plan.

The challenge we discuss in the following chapter is how to respond quickly — ideally, within your first hundred days — when you begin to realize that you've taken a wrong turn on your career path and should change jobs. Yes, you'll experience some short-term disruption when this happens. But making a course correction now could save you many wasted years in a job that just makes you miserable.

CHAPTER 11

Satisfaction: Graceful Exits

"The only way to do great work is to love the work you do."
—Steve Jobs

You wake up one morning with a sinking feeling. "I've made a terrible mistake," you say to your bathroom mirror. "This job isn't going to work."

Your first instinct might be to tough it out. "Work isn't supposed to be fun. I have a life outside this job... friends, family, things I love to do. And it won't look good if I quit a job just a month or two after I started."

Well, maybe that's true.

But sadly, most of the time a job you don't love doesn't get any better. You just dig yourself in deeper, becoming more unhappy as time goes by. You also become the kind of disgruntled employee that your boss wants to replace and your team members don't trust. When you do finally move on, finding a better job becomes really hard.

In fact, a remarkable high percentage of employees, both new hires and veterans, get virtually no satisfaction from their jobs. An ongoing Gallup survey of workplace trends found that more than two-thirds of U.S. employees are either "not engaged" (51.0%) or "actively disengaged" (17.5%) in their jobs. In effect, says Gallup, these disengaged employees are sleepwalking through their workday, putting time—but not energy or passion—into their work.

Moreover, the Gallup data shows that the least-engaged workers tend to be the notorious Millennials, the most recent entrants into the workforce. The explanation, says Gallup, is mostly economic: "Although the economy is improving, workers in this generation may not be getting the jobs they had hoped for coming out of college [or] may not be working in jobs that allow them to use their talents and strengths."

Yet when you think about it, the high percentage of employees who dislike their jobs is hard to explain just in terms of job scarcity. Presumably, most of these "disengaged" employees were picked after a highly selective filtering process (hundreds or even thousands of qualified applicants, dozens of finalists who were even more carefully screened). Their future colleagues and bosses spent hours interviewing the best candidates, told them about the company culture and the work they'd be doing, and followed up on their references. How could so many apparent winners turn into a "bad fit" for their jobs?

Here's at least part of the answer: Our current recruiting process is badly flawed. Swamped by applicants, companies now focus more than ever on credentials and skills (which are easy to quantify) and pay little attention to character, motivation, and cultural fit (which are hard to define, not to mention difficult to quantify). And more than ever, HR departments and recruiters are overwhelmed with look-alike resumes. According to one recent research study, resume readers now spend an average of only *six seconds* skimming through an individual resume before deciding to keep reading or toss it.

If your resume does happen to make the cut, you get to advance to the next phase: A face-to-face interview with managers and other staff members who are likely to be clueless about the qualities that predict success in their own company's work environment. Have the people who interview you been trained to ask penetrating questions about motivation, character, engagement? Do they know the two or three red-flag answers that identify potential sleepwalkers and malcontents? Unlikely.

No surprise: This assembly-line process fills job slots with thousands of talented C++ programmers, Ivy League grads, and charming sales reps, few of whom have any enthusiasm for the values and culture of their new workplace. (One especially harsh critic said, "Using HR as talent spotters makes about as much sense as asking the florist for help filling out the roster on your basketball team.")

Is this an exaggeration? Here's how Laszlo Bock, Google's senior vice president for people operations, described the results of an internal analysis of his company's widely-admired recruiting process:

> We did a study to determine whether anyone at Google is particularly good at hiring. We looked at tens of thousands of interviews, and everyone who had done the interviews and what they scored the candidate, and how that person ultimately performed in their job. We found zero relationship. It's a complete random mess, except for one guy who was highly predictive because he only interviewed people for a very specialized area, where he happened to be the world's leading expert.

Now, it's possible that Google's "complete random mess" is nothing more than a symptom of one company's sloppy recruiting process. Maybe Google didn't deserve to be ranked by Fortune as the country's #1 "best company to work for" for five separate years. Maybe the real professionals could do better...

As it happens, Heidrick & Struggles, one of the country's largest executive recruiting firms, revealed its own scorecard a few years ago for 20,000 senior executive placements — presumably, a universe of hiring decisions that reflect the HR industry's most expert efforts to make successful matchups.

The results? H&S found that 40% of the new senior-level executives it placed were "pushed out, failed or quit" within 18 months of being hired. Oops.

So don't feel badly if your wonderful new job isn't working out. You're not alone.

What do you do when you realize you're not the right person for the job you just barely started?

First, identify the source of your greatest pain. Your boss is a jackass? Your job description was a total lie? The stress level is overwhelming? You're underpaid, treated rudely, or ignored when you ask about career opportunities? The cafeteria is run by a soup Nazi?

Your goal here is to move from being a victim ("my job is terrible") to taking charge of your career. Be as specific as possible—in fact, make a point of writing down your top pain issues and taking notes on events and conversations that demonstrate the problem. Then, see if you can come up with a few practical ideas for improving your current job situation.

What you *may* find is that some of your toughest satisfaction issues can be fixed... sometimes by simple patience (waiting for a seasonal crunch to end), sometimes by a transfer to a different department, sometimes just by insisting on better treatment. Remember that from your new company's perspective, you represent a non-trivial investment of time and money. Rather than see you walk out the door, the managers who hired you may make a good faith effort to salvage the situation.

A typical scenario:

Betsy is a talented graphic designer who joined an ad agency to develop packaging concepts for the agency's clients. Package design was Betsy's dream job, but she came to dread dealing with the agency's highly demanding and sometimes abusive clients. Ready to quit, she timidly asked her new boss if her job could be redefined to eliminate face-to-face client presentations. "Heck, yes," said her boss. "Our account guys get paid well enough to handle those knuckleheads. I'd much rather have you spend time on the creative stuff that you're so good at."

Of course, there's no guarantee that your new company will be this helpful. They may be delighted to get rid of you. They may need you—or someone like you—to do the stuff you hate. Or the boss's idiot nephew covets your job. Or you know it's going to take more than a few management concessions to make the company's toxic work environment bearable.

At this point, you know you *have* to leave.

Nevertheless, don't just walk out the door. Bear in mind that future employers are going to wonder about the job you abruptly abandoned after two or three months. Without a doubt, your departure is going to be a big question mark, and they'll certainly talk to anyone at your old company they can reach. The story you want them to hear goes something like this: "Betsy was a fabulous designer—a real star. We wanted to hang on to her, but she had to work with a few pretty rough clients who happen to pay our bills. Believe me, you'd be lucky to have her in your shop."

Naturally, you should also do your best to make your departure as painless as possible for your company. Don't bail a week before a major trade show or product ship date. Don't leave a drawer full of unfinished reports, illegible notes, and unpaid invoices. Be sure to tell your clients and vendors that you're leaving, and introduce them to their interim contact person (you can certainly mention that you're job hunting — you may pick up some useful leads).

How long should you hang around? That's always a judgment call. It may be company policy to kick you out the day you give notice, and to cancel your company email and change the locks as soon as you exit the building. More often, you'll have at least a few weeks at full pay to help with the transition, and perhaps even more time with no paycheck but with free use of an office and a phone. You might even set up a consulting or free-lance relationship. Find out what the company's standard arrangements are before you announce that you're leaving, so you're not caught by surprise.

Finally, before you walk, make sure your relationship with your boss is solid. Ask for a letter of reference, and be sure you can list your boss as a reference. As much as you can, make sure that your work history is entirely positive when future employers run a background check.

'The Devil Wears Prada': Finding a Job You Love

So you're unemployed... again. Here's the first thing you should *not* do: Fire off a barrage of resumes to every possible employer on your old prospect list. Remember: That's the approach that landed you in a job you ended up hating. You need a Plan B.

Strange as it may sound, this might be a good time to visit (or re-visit) a classic movie called *The Devil Wears Prada*. The plot line: Andrea Sachs (Anne Hathaway) is a small-town girl who comes to New York hoping to launch a career as a journalist. Instead, she gets sidetracked by a job as an assistant to Miranda Priestly (Meryl Streep), the fearsome and influential editor of a Vogue-like fashion magazine. Despite Miranda's abuse and nit-picking, Andrea manages to become a rising star in the world of fashion publishing... and eventually wins her boss's grudging respect. At which point Andrea decides to abandon her glamorous new career and finds true happiness as a reporter on a small newspaper.

The point, of course, is that it's not always enough to be an on-the-job success or to enjoy the reflected glory of a famous company. *Your own job satisfaction also matters—a lot.* If there's one lesson a bad job can teach you, it's the importance of finding a job that makes you feel good about what you're doing.

"I tried that, and it doesn't work," a reader protests. "I'm passionate about eliminating world hunger. Nobody will hire me to do that job."

No, they probably won't. It's wonderful whenever you can find a job that engages your passion... but passion is usually a rather private matter. The term we use here, deliberately, is "job satisfaction." Satisfaction is the feeling you get from your day-to-day work—the way you interact with your colleagues, the tasks you perform, the rewards you earn, the skills and knowledge you learn, the sense of fairness, security, respect, and excitement that your job conveys.

Author Cal Newport makes a similar point when he argues that the "passion hypothesis" — the popular theory that career success depends on aligning your passion with your job — is simply bad advice:

> [The passion hypothesis] not only fails to describe how most people actually end up with compelling careers, but for many people it can actually make things worse: leading to chronic job shifting and unrelenting angst when one's reality inevitably falls short of the dream...

> The things that make a great job great, I discovered, are rare and valuable. If you want them in your working life, you need something rare and valuable to offer in return. In other words, you need to be good at something before you can expect a good job.

As Newport points out, many people derive great satisfaction from quite ordinary jobs that most people wouldn't find exciting or inspiring. Meanwhile, plenty of people land in dream jobs that they felt passionate about at first—only to find that the noble-sounding non-profit agency they joined is a living hell for its employees, or that a glamorous acting career demands endless casting calls and rejections. Passion and satisfaction are simply different experiences.

But here's the hard part: Discovering what gives each of us the greatest job satisfaction tends to be a long and very personal learning process. Chester Elton, the author of *What Motivates Me,* says his own research reveals that "each individual is driven by a unique set, or blend, of internal and external drivers. Every person on this planet has a thumbprint-like makeup of what makes him most happy 9-5 (and in the rest of life); and those thumbprints vary considerably."

You've probably gained a few insights from your first hundred days on a new job. But that's almost certainly not enough raw data to define the next 20 years of your career. And don't discount the impact of purely random events, sometimes known as "luck." Dilbert cartoonist Scott Adams says he spent many years working (and often failing) "at a long series of day jobs and entrepreneurial adventures," including eight years slowly climbing the career ladder at a large San Francisco bank. Becoming a cartoonist was almost an accident, he admits:

> Dilbert started out as just one of many get-rich schemes I was willing to try. When it started to look as if it might be a success, my passion for cartooning increased because I realized it could be my golden ticket. In hindsight, it looks as if the projects that I was most passionate about were also the ones that worked. But objectively, my passion level moved with my success. Success caused passion more than passion caused success.

Scott Adams also points out that his pre-Dilbert career wasn't entirely trial-and-error. Adams had a rough sense of where he wanted his life to go: he was willing to take risks, he was eager to learn, and he "wanted to create, invent, write, or otherwise concoct something widely desired that would be easy to

118

reproduce." That was enough self-knowledge to put his career on the right path.

So hold off the frenzied search for a new job for a week or two. Instead, take time to think about the kind of job that will make you feel good about work, about yourself, about your future. It may take a while to get there... but at least you'll be moving in the right direction.

Toward that end, here's a brief self-assessment quiz that might give you some useful insights:

Your Job Satisfaction Profile
....

When you're interviewing for a job, you're bound to hear questions about the "fit" between you and the company. That's an important conversation: Employers have found that a mismatch between their culture and the candidate's needs almost always leads to poor morale and low job satisfaction. And unhappy employees rarely produce top results, regardless of their technical skills.

But predicting a "good fit" is a tough question for both the employer and the would-be employee. Employers tend to take a fairly simple top-down approach that often reflects the CEO's self-image ("We offer a challenging, creative environment and highly competitive incentives"). Meanwhile, the poor candidate rarely has much insight into his or her personal satisfaction goals ("Who cares what I want? Just tell me the answer that gets me the job"). A few months later, everybody is disappointed.

What creates high job satisfaction?

For most employees, there are three broad factors that impact satisfaction — **Cash** (money and other financial incentives), **Community** (a friendly, supportive work environment), and **Contacts** (access to high-profile people and opportunities). However, hardly anyone cares *equally* about these goals: For some employees, money is everything, while others derive satisfaction primarily from being part of a team or a social group. And still others would gladly work for free in a hellish environment in order to gain access to the right opportunities.

Of course, we'd all like a career path that delivered piles of cash, wonderful co-workers, and a shot at becoming a super-star. These jobs do exist, but no surprise — they're incredibly competitive and often

119

demand all-consuming dedication to the job at the expense of your work-life balance.

Thus, the most practical career question you probably face is simply to clarify your own priorities. We created this brief set of questions to help you define the career goals that you should try to maximize in your job search (and if you discover your present job is a terrible fit with those priorities, to get you thinking seriously about moving on).

Instructions: First, for each of the following statements about yourself, assign a score of 1, 2, or 3:

> 1 = *doesn't matter*
> 2 = *nice if it happens*
> 3 = *a big deal for me*

Then add up the total scores for each category and see what the numbers reveal about your overall personal priorities.

Finally, go through the individual statements and circle the two or three "big deal" items that are **most important to you.**

CASH

My goal is to make a lot more money than my peers, preferably within the next five years.
Score: _____

It's important for me to have a reliable, steady source of income.
Score: _____

I'd like to have a chance to make money outside of my regular job.
Score: _____

I expect substantial raises (merit- or seniority-based) as part of my comp plan.
Score: _____

I expect substantial retirement benefits as part of my comp plan.
Score: _____

TOTAL _____

COMMUNITY

I get great satisfaction as part of a work-related team.
Score: _____

I get great satisfaction from interacting with our clients and customers.
Score: _____

I want to be part of a company with an excellent reputation.
Score: _____

It's very important to me that all employees are treated fairly and with respect.
Score: _____

I want to work with people who are likely to become my after-hours friends.
Score: _____

TOTAL _____

CONTACTS

In my chosen career, success depends heavily on credentials (e.g., degrees from specific colleges, jobs with leading firms).
Score: _____

I expect that my job will provide many of the skills and expertise that I now lack.
Score: _____

I expect that my job will provide me with industry contacts, visibility, and respect.
Score: _____

I want my boss to play an active mentoring role in advancing my career.
Score: _____

I want a company that honors my accomplishments.
Score: _____

TOTAL _____

Interpreting Your Results

Most people will report *roughly* the same number of 1's, 2's, and 3's in their responses.

If almost all of your responses are 1's and 2's, that's likely to be a sign that you lack interest in work of any kind. You may have trouble finding a job that really inspires you, and your performance level may be relatively poor... so your ideal job might be low in stress, with well-defined tasks.

At the other extreme, too many 3's may indicate that you're unrealistic about your dream job and have trouble defining your own top priorities. Be careful about weighing multiple job offers (a nice problem to have, of course), because most of the jobs you're offered will have some "ideal" qualities.

Identifying your top two or three "most important" statements may take some thought, but these are the critical personal issues that you should raise when you interview for future jobs. If you don't get good answers from a prospective employer on these issues, that's a sign that the job probably won't be a good fit for you.

★

Successful Search Tips

As you probably noticed, the world is full of advice on how to land your dream job... but not much about what to do when you're back on the street, looking for a second chance. Do you just hit the big red Reset button and start over? No.

Some useful tactics to leverage your admittedly limited on-the-job experience:

 Don't waste time on jobs that will make you unhappy: Pay close attention to the negative factors in your ideal career path. For instance, working for a big law firm is challenging and well paid—but the stress level is high and you'll probably work brutally long hours to reach your quota of billable hours. If that kind of environment makes you miserable, look for a job that requires your legal skills but provides a more satisfying environment (perhaps a corporate legal department, a government agency, or a law school). And if you're completely turned off by a whole industry or profession, don't despair: You almost certainly have *some* skills and education that will give you a leg up in a brand-new line of work.

 Reposition your resume: As a general rule, avoid overly-general job categories like "administrative assistant" and "software developer". Yes, there will be lots of companies that list such openings—but you'll also be competing against huge numbers of candidates, too. You're better off revising your resume to emphasize a more specialized focus—for instance, as a "researcher" (if you've spent four years writing college term papers, that's legitimate on-the-job-training) or as an "e-commerce Web site developer" (if you've helped a friend create an online order form for her t-shirt company, you'll have a working

122

sample of your work). Most importantly, having a defined focus sends a message to potential employers that you'll be enthusiastic about *their* specific project. That immediately sets you apart from all the I'll-do-anything generalists.

✓ **Start upgrading your credentials:** In recent years, employers have gone nuts over credentials and certifications, and they'll bounce your resume if you're not already an MBA, a Microsoft certified network administrator, an intensive care nurse, or a licensed hairdresser. However... some employers will hire you (perhaps at a more entry-level job) if you're currently enrolled in a program that leads to the necessary credential. You'll have to juggle school and a full-time job for a year or two, but at the end you'll have both the educational credential *and* real job experience.

✓ **Build your resume with part-time work:** While you're searching for a new job, actively solicit consulting gigs, free-lance assignments, temp work, and even volunteer projects that will enhance your otherwise skimpy resume. If you've positioned yourself as a "researcher" or "e-commerce Web site developer," for instance, you'll look much more credible if you've just completed three different projects that fit this description. And of course you'll get a chance to show off your talents to potential employers and sources of references.

✓ **Cut your overhead:** A lot of bad job decisions are made because out-of-work people need immediate cash to pay their bills. That's a realistic problem, so look for ways to take away some of the pressure. Get a roommate. Don't charge small (or large) luxuries on your credit cards. Eliminate your daily visits to Starbucks. And as Henry David Thoreau once said, "beware of all enterprises that require new clothes" — in other words, no wardrobe makeover until you actually get a paycheck.

Here's Marina Shifrin, famous for an "I quit" video message to her boss that went viral on YouTube, on being a cheapskate:

Your twenties are for living like a poor person; comfort shouldn't be a priority. When I first moved to New York City after college, I smuggled flasks into bars to avoid pricey drinks (thanks, double-D's!) and I never went out to eat or bought nice clothes. I was following my parents' lead—even after becoming successful business owners, they continued to shop at Walmart. My friends didn't love it when I skipped birthday dinners, and I went without the Internet for a couple of months, but I never, ever had to stress about making rent.

✓ **Finally, talk to the people who didn't hire you the first time:** Remember the jobs where you got as far as an interview... and then didn't make the final cut? Like you, the candidate who won the gold ring may also be leaving. As a runner-up, you're an especially attractive and pre-screened replacement. Career and job search counselor J. T. O'Donnell says it's helpful to remember that "'No' doesn't always mean 'never'—it often means 'not today.'"

Smart job seekers understand hiring situations in a company can change overnight. They put aside their pride and show their professionalism to the employer by staying in touch. Just recently, I worked with a woman who interviewed not once, but two times with a company. Both times they went with another candidate. However, the third time they called and directly hired her for a new position without even interviewing her for it. Why? They already knew she could do the job from the previous two rounds of interviews. Better still, in her own words, 'The role was perfect for me. Much better than the first two jobs I applied for.' And the job paid more, too.

★

The Path of the Lone Wolf

Here's how Steve Wozniak, the revered inventor of the Apple personal computer, describes a personal style that's often in conflict with the collaborative thinking that dominates modern companies and institutions:

> Most inventors and engineers I've met are like me—they're shy and they live in their heads. They're almost like artists. In fact, the very best of them are artists. And artists work best alone where they can control an invention's design without a lot of other people designing it for marketing or some other committee. I don't believe anything really revolutionary has been invented by a committee. If you're that rare engineer who's an inventor and also an artist, I'm going to give you some advice that might be hard to take. That advice is: work alone. You're going to be best able to design revolutionary products and features if you're working on your own. Not on a committee. Not on a team.

For some employees—frequently, those with exceptional talents and skills—working in a corporate environment feels like an unnatural act. "I react like a solitary wolf who's trying to live with a pack of domesticated dogs," one unhappy manager says. "The others play well together, but I just snarl at everybody."

Lone wolves tend to function best in jobs with minimal collaboration and few team handoffs, and that's a fact of life you should take seriously if you're re-thinking your career path. The "bad fit" in your current job may not be the fault of the jerks you're forced to work with—it's possible that *your* personal style is the main source of your frustration.

If you're just starting your career, you may not even realize that you're a genuine lone wolf. Since lone wolves are usually high performers, moreover, you may start out as a rising star, in line for a fast-track promotion to a managerial job.

And that's when you may start running into trouble. Lone wolves make lousy bosses: They tend to be perfectionists, they dislike delegating, they may behave rudely in meetings, and they quickly lose faith in the motives and competence of their company's senior management. The faster they rise, the less happy they become.

Lone wolves tend to be *least* comfortable in companies that rely on "closed" teams (see Chapter 3) and extensive collaboration; they also have little patience with highly paternalistic company cultures. When you start looking for your next job, avoid any opportunities that look like this. You probably won't prosper.

But aside from these negatives, what should you actively look for? Broadly speaking, there are three major career paths for lone wolves:

Path #1: The specialist track: Traditional career paths are almost always based on promotions to successively higher levels of management. That's bad news for employees who dislike managing other people and want to keep doing the hands-on work they enjoy—for instance, classroom teachers, programmers, sales reps, reporters, administrative assistants, scientists, on and on. They may earn modest raises based on seniority, but relatively few organizations have figured out how to create a promotion track just for specialists who mostly work alone. When you run across a company that *does* have such a track, put any job leads on your top-priority contact list.

Path #2: Self-employment: For better or worse, the U.S. economy seems to be moving away from full-time jobs to a heavier reliance on part-timers, contract workers, and free-lancers. Self-employment is not an attractive path for people without marketable skills... but higher-skilled self-employed people tend to end up with more income and much greater job satisfaction than their full-time counterparts. Of course, you'll have to figure out how to market yourself, how to juggle multiple projects, and how to turn a profit. But those are skills you should master for just about any career path.

Path #3: Your own company: As you might expect, startups and small businesses have great appeal for lone wolf personalities. At least in theory, the boss always gets to make the "right" decisions with minimal pushback from employees, and the profits aren't wasted on unproductive overhead. However, the risks are also high, especially if you don't have experience running a small business. If you've just left your first real job, a safer path might be to *start* with self-employment and gradually transform your solo practice into a multi-employee or multi-partner company. Starting your own company is fairly easy; escaping from a startup you own that's in zombie-land is much harder.

PART II

Personal Stories

When I began writing *The First Hundred Days*, something curious happened: Many of my friends and family members who heard about the book immediately launched into stories about their own first jobs. "Aha!" I said to myself. "They're not just being polite. That first-job experience really does have a life-long impact on people's lives." (Trade secret: The usual response when a writer talks about a new book project is "How very nice. So how about those Red Sox?")

I also realized that the personal stories I was hearing provided a very different perspective on *The First Hundred Days* theme. The book I originally planned was largely a traditional how-to guide—straight practical advice, usually based on insights from expert observers and researchers. The stories I was hearing were more intense, more anecdotal, more like folk wisdom. The storytellers weren't offering career advice—they were talking about their own lives.

So... I created a separate home in *The First Hundred Days* just for personal narratives. In the pages that follow, I've assembled first-person stories that reflect a broad range of first-job experiences and success strategies, across many kinds of jobs and companies. If you're curious about what a first-time job *feels* like—here are some great revelations.

—Jeffrey Tarter

"Silver Dolphins"

The Submarine Warfare Insignia (nicknamed "Silver Dolphins") is a badge worn only by fully qualified submariners. As part of the Silver Dolphins qualification process, junior sailors must learn about every system on their sub, from the nuclear reactor that turns the screw to the CO_2 scrubbers that recycle the air to the water purification system that turns sewage into drinkable water. Junior sailors (called Nubs, short for "Non-Useful Bodies") also get trained on damage control skills, so they can snuff out fires, stop leaks, and fight off hostile takeovers.

Of course, rookie Nubs start out knowing very little about what it takes to be a submariner. So they get tasked with most of the sub's janitorial work.

That's what happened when I joined the sub's crew for my first deployment. I got the standard Nub assignment — washing dishes in the galley for my first month onboard. During that time, I'd have to wear a pointy paper hat and a red t-shirt. Supposedly, this outfit is a lesson in humility: the rest of the crew could tell immediately that I wasn't qualified to do much except clean.

When I started my first shift in the galley, I found I'd be working in a closet-sized scullery compartment. That wasn't too bad... but almost immediately the boat started moving out towards the deep part of the ocean. Then a storm rolled in. Subs are designed to go underwater but we were still on the surface, so the boat started rocking port and starboard like crazy. I remember chasing the dishes around on the counter as they slid back and forth. It must have been a pretty funny scene, in a Groucho Marx kind of way — though I was far too queasy to laugh at the time. The constant side-to-side rocking made my head hurt and the half-chewed strips of meat floating in the murky sink around the pile of greasy plates churned my stomach.

I caught up with the plates, rinsed them off and slammed them into the circular metal washing machine. The racket drew the attention of a senior sailor in my division, FT2 Livingston. "Hey, Munkachy," he yelled. "It gets better, shipmate."

I forced a fake grin. It was my first day on the boat, and already I was sick of hearing that word: shipmate. I didn't feel like anyone's shipmate. I felt more like a slave. I kept slamming the dishes around. I didn't want to admit it to anyone, but I was pissed off. I didn't sign up for submarines to wipe slop off of plates. I was a Fire Control Technician. I was supposed to be in the control room, interpreting sonar data and providing the Officer of the Deck with course suggestions—not back here in the galley with the Culinary Specialists.

We finally submerged, and the boat eventually stopped rocking and rolling. But at the end of lunchtime, the crew shoved in even more plates and silverware for me to wash as they made their way to their respective watch stations.

By the end of the shift I was covered in kitchen slime and hating life. Still, I had no other choice—I had to suck it up and keep scrubbing away for at least another month. When my relief finally arrived, I went to the head (Navy term for bathroom) to wash up. On a submarine, there is a limited supply of water in the tanks, so everyone takes really quick showers—no more than five minutes long. Two minutes into my rinse, a shipmate pounded on the stall door and told me to hurry the f**k up and get out of there. "Hollywood showers are not authorized, Nub!"

And thus began my first hundred days underway on a nuclear submarine. As I struggled to wash up and get out, the truth hit me: I was trapped in a giant sardine can with about 180 disgruntled sailors. There was no way out, save through the escape hatch. The one and only way to better my situation was to earn my Silver Dolphins.

That awful first day set the tone for the rest of my first underway deployment. Thanks to an ambitious slave-driver captain, morale was in the pits before we even set out on our three-month mission. Our rotund, leathery silent leader hailed from the Cherokee nation and was about as tough as they come. He could live on two hours sleep a day and he expected the rest of the crew to keep up with the manly drill schedule he had planned out.

"Attention helm, dive, quartermaster!" the captain would bellow as he entered the control room, often unexpectedly. "I am the captain and I have the deck and the conn."

It wasn't unusual for the captain to run an unscheduled drill if he was bored. One drill, called "emergency blow," was designed to test the ship's ability to surface quickly in an emergency. During this drill, the ship would rise at extreme angles, causing everyone who was trying to get some sleep to roll out of their racks.

Our captain seemed to fancy himself as a throwback to the WWII submarine captains of yore. He never grew tired. He never seemed unsure of himself. He seldom laughed. If he did laugh, it was a really loud laugh that scared the heck out of everyone. Our XO (Executive Officer) was of the same species as our captain: a square-jawed, rectangular-headed, stern-faced taskmaster with an imposing presence and a booming voice.

Your grandmother puckers her lips before she kisses you, but on a submarine the word "pucker" is used to describe what happens at the other end of the body in stressful situations. The captain's silent presence alone was enough to increase the crew's pucker factor tenfold. A seemingly innocuous eyebrow raise after a less-than-perfect drill could spell yet another "Vulcan death watch" drill cycle for the entire crew. Nobody wanted to be "that guy" — the crewmember who ruined it all for everyone by saying or doing something stupid. By the time the Tactical Readiness Exam rolled around, the crew were so puckered up that they were practically biting donuts out of their seat cushions. Clipboard-holders from the pentagon loomed over their shoulders, watching and evaluating, clicking their pens and sucking their teeth.

Meanwhile, while all the senior sailors were getting tested, my task was to wash dishes and scurry around the ship in my stinky red t-shirt and collect qualification card signatures in my off-time. After about a month of galley duty, I became a messenger — an ever-so-slightly more dignified job. The messenger's main job is to deliver first, second and third wake up calls to the oncoming watch section. His second mission is to refill coffee cups.

Waking up a junior sailor is easy. The standard way to do it is to flip on the overhead light and say "first wake up." Then you wait a few minutes and do the same thing again, only you say "second wake up." Waking up the officers, though, requires a little more formality and finesse. The most nervewracking moment of my shift came when it was time to wake up the captain.

The captain and the XO are the only two individuals on board a sub who enjoy the luxury of private accommodations. When venturing into the captain's stateroom, I often felt like I was tiptoeing into a cave to wake up a bear.

The captain's wake up call had to be delivered in just the right way, using a traditional litany reserved only for waking up the boat's commanding officer. If I fumbled over the words, I'd look like an idiot. The first time I delivered the captain's wake up, I had to mumble the wakeup litany to myself about a million times until I knew the words by heart. Often he was already awake, just laying there with his eyes open in the dark.

Life improved after I got out of the galley, but the crew's morale took a turn for the worse during a particularly unpleasant sound-silencing exercise. During sound-silencing exercises, all the metal doors on the ship are removed and replaced with brown sheets of plastic Naugahyde to dampen noise. Somebody had decided to cut up some of the Naugahyde flaps with a knife—probably in retaliation for all the excessive drilling we were doing, or at least that's how our captain saw it. The captain took the vandalism personally and ordered all the Naugahyde to be rolled up and stowed away. As a result, for the rest of the week-long sound-silencing exercise we had to defecate and urinate in front of each other like animals.

If you can find a way to laugh, you can make it through the first hundred days of any stressful job. Emergency room doctors use gallows humor to get through the day because their job involves facing death on a daily basis. Submariners, on the other hand, deal with disgusting stuff every day—cramped compartments, relentless burping and farting, bilge slime, smelly hydraulic oil— so we tend to have a gross sense of humor. During the no-

Naugahyde days, I was once tasked with scrubbing the deck area in front of the head. I have a distinct unpleasant memory of my shipmate sitting on the john just a few feet away while I scrubbed the floor with a sponge. He took the opportunity to give me a play-by-play of the action, using a sports announcer cadence. Gross humor is how we got through gross situations.

The mysterious Naugahyde knifer never came forward to admit his guilt, so the punishments grew worse and worse. All divisions were assigned pointless cleaning tasks and the drill schedule got even more hectic. Later we received even more bad news: we were getting extended. Normally, a deployment is ninety days long. However, the submarine that was set to relieve us had run into some difficulties getting ready. As a result, we were going to have to stay out an extra two weeks. The extension meant that in addition to missing Christmas, we were also going to have to celebrate New Years on the submarine instead of with our families.

The crew's misery made getting my Silver Dolphins that much more difficult. Despite my relentless efforts, I initially wasn't very successful at getting my shipmates to teach me about their jobs. The harder I tried to impress, the more determined they were to give me a hard time. I couldn't understand what I was doing wrong, so at first I let their resistance and skepticism get to me. I began to think that I wasn't cut out to be a sailor. I went into a dish-washing trance and started hitting the rack right after my shift instead of studying or learning from my shipmates. It wasn't long before I started falling behind.

My mindset began to change after I got out of my own head. Once I learned enough about submarine life to put myself in my shipmates' position, I could see that to the crew I was just an anxious looking guy who smelled of stale beef stroganoff, standing there holding a wrinkled piece of paper — nothing but a serious-faced, miserable-looking, pushy Nub in need of ink. Helping me in my studies wasn't anyone's priority because my red-eyed shipmates had problems of their own. In addition to Captain Ahab and our Frankenstein XO, there were also maintenance tasks to complete, wrenches to turn, paperwork to fill out.

But it wasn't just that my shipmates were tired and busy. There was also another reason why they were reluctant to sign my card—the deeper political situation surrounding the qualification process itself. If at any point it should turn out that a Nub doesn't actually know anything about a particular system despite having the required signature for it, the senior guy who gave him the signature is the one who takes the heat. The tense mood that permeated the boat during my first underway made it hard to get someone to go out on a limb and sign my card.

As the days rolled on I discovered that getting qualified isn't just about decoding complicated manuals and memorizing numbers and diagrams. It's also about earning respect and trust. Showing up during the midwatch (midnight to 6:00 in the morning) a few times when nothing important was going on paid off. Hanging out made my shipmates feel more comfortable with me, and that comfort led to trust. I found little ways to make myself useful by running to get tools or by helping out with post-watch cleanups and I soaked up knowledge by watching and listening to what was going on. After my shipmates realized that I wasn't going to wash out, I started to accumulate signatures.

During the last part of the final qualifications, I had to respond to emergency situations in front of the captain, the XO, and the Chief of the Boat. The day before, I stayed up almost my entire off-watch going over procedures and memorizing the words I would need to use to call in emergencies over the 1MC. To say I was nervous would be putting it mildly.

By then I knew that very few Silver Dolphins candidates actually fail badly enough to get sent to the surface fleet. Like many of the rituals that people encounter in high-pressure occupations, the Silver Dolphins qualification process is more of an initiation than it is a test. Still, even though repeating the test is nearly always an option, messing up could mean a massive loss of cool points and respect. Major mistakes become jokes that are hard to live down. Nobody wants to be the guy who hooked up the submersible pump the wrong way during a flooding drill.

So there I was, performing in front of the top brass. I relied on a mental trick that helped me grind through endless piles of dirty dishes: I reminded myself to slow down and focus completely on only one thing at a time. Because I didn't occupy my mind with thoughts of making mistakes, I didn't freak out when the straps on my Emergency Air Breather mask got tangled up during a fire drill. I was able to recover and don the mask in the required amount of time by forcing myself to forget about everything else except for the problem at hand.

Of course, practicing ahead of time and familiarizing myself with all the damage control gear in my free time also helped. Also, gleaning knowledge from recently qualified guys enabled me to get the inside scoop on the type of obstacles the captain liked to include on the test. Because I was well prepared, there were no big surprises and I managed to make it through without embarrassing myself.

I remember vividly how good I felt after the whole thing was over. For the very first time, I was allowed to sip "bug juice" (Kool-Aid) and watch a movie in the Crew's Lounge with the rest of my Silver Dolphins shipmates. A few days rolled by and before I knew it, I was standing in front of the crew while the captain pinned on my fish badge. I was a qualified submariner at last.

Alex Munkachy
Budapest, Hungary

"I was... interesting"

Back when personal computers were the hottest new idea, 13-year-old Jonathan Rotenberg founded the Boston Computer Society. The BCS (whose first meeting space was the cafeteria in young Jonathan's high school) quickly became the country's biggest and most influential PC user group. Computer and software companies routinely launched major products at BCS meetings, and Jonathan's personal network grew to include most of the emerging high-tech industry's top CEOs and other movers and shakers.

Jonathan went on to add a few other credentials, including an MBA degree from Harvard Business School and a summer internship with a prestigious management consulting firm. A year later, he joined the firm, Cambridge-based Monitor Group, as a full-time employee.

We asked Jonathan to talk about what happened next:

Since I'd already worked at Monitor as an intern, I knew my way around and I'd met a lot of the people there. What surprised me was that my experience as an entrepreneur – a pretty successful entrepreneur – didn't seem to count for much. It had zero impact on my salary negotiations, and the consultants I was working with didn't understand the fast-moving high-tech world that I came from. To them, I was… interesting. That was about all.

Consulting companies are all about billable hours, so almost immediately I was assigned to a project team with 25 other consultants. The client was a multi-billion dollar aluminum conglomerate that was trying to raise its valuation on Wall Street. The company's old strategy had been to vertically integrate 190 separate business units that did everything from digging aluminum ore out of the ground to making aluminum cans for soda companies. The job of the Monitor team was to analyze each of these 190 business units and create ten-year forecasts for their individual growth, profitability, price competition, tax incentives, and global markets. The aluminum company could then use these forecasts to decide which businesses to divest and which businesses would contribute the most value in the future.

My piece of this project was to act as the "modeler," the guy who would build a giant Excel spreadsheet model that could link all the numbers together. I thought this was a very interesting, very cool problem – the kind of thing that attracted me to management consulting in the first place.

By the time I was done, I'd designed and built a monster spreadsheet made up of 1,500 individual worksheets. Someone told me that I'd probably set a world record for the biggest single spreadsheet model. Pretty good for a rookie MBA.

But the project was getting out of control. Each of the 190 business units had a general manager whose whole career depended on the performance of his group. When our consultants predicted that individual businesses weren't going to be an asset to the company, the general managers fought back.

The Monitor team was constantly putting out fires, recalculating forecasts, and fending off attacks on our credibility.

And inevitably, we did make mistakes. I remember going over the numbers behind a presentation that was due the next day, and suddenly discovered that I'd left out *a billion dollars* in revenue. I ran down the hall to my boss and told him the bad news. His face went white—though we managed to fix the presentation in time. But that's the sort of thing that happens when you're dealing with thousands and thousands of numbers in a spreadsheet.

Naturally, keeping up with our original schedule was becoming brutally hard. I was putting in eighty to ninety hours a week, not sleeping, desperate to avoid mistakes. At one point my boss took a good look at me and said, "Go home. Get some sleep before you come back."

And then Monitor dropped a *second* project on my plate. In theory, Monitor consultants were supposed to devote no more than 50% of their time to an individual client. The company had landed a major strategy project with AT&T and I seemed to be underutilized, so...

By then, I could see that the pressure would never let up. I'd been warned that consulting companies like Monitor routinely burn out most of their new hires. My goal had been to survive at least two years, and in the end I lasted about three and a half. That was enough.

Jonathan Rotenberg
Boston, MA

"As invisible as wallpaper"

I don't remember exactly why, but when I was ten years old I decided that it would be cool to be a Congressional page. I later found out that being a page is a tough job to land. You have to go through a pretty rigorous application process *and* be recommended by a senator (for the Senate pages) or a congressman (for the House pages). So in my sophomore year in high school, I fired off applications to every senator whose Web site had an application. John Kerry, who was one of my own state's senators, finally came through just in time for me to join the pages who were accepted for the first semester of my junior year.

Being a congressional page is an amazing opportunity if you're interested in a career in politics or government. Pages race around the Capitol delivering messages and documents, they run errands, and they do personal favors for almost everyone from Congressional movers-and-shakers to the hundreds of staffers who actually write most of the legislation that Congress votes on. Many of the big shots simply ignore you, but you do meet plenty of nice people who might be a help later on in your career.

You also get to hang out with 30 or so other pages from all over the country, who all live in a big dormitory and attend classes together during their four-month internships. Of course, almost everyone is a political geek, so it's not unusual to take part in a riotous debate in the cafeteria about a passage in *Robert's Rules of Order.* Great fun!

Unfortunately, it's also really hard to stand out with so much competition. When I started my gig as a Senate page, I realized right away that being a page makes you almost as invisible as wallpaper. We all wore the same blue uniforms (including the same ugly black orthopedic shoes), we all lived in the same dormitories, and we all worked for the same boss (the Sergeant at Arms). One hair out of place or a wrinkled shirt and you'd be sent straight back to the dorm for a makeover.

I knew I wanted to come on strong, so I applied for a quasi-supervisory role as the "floor page" for my shift. The floor page sends pages off to pick up documents elsewhere in the building, keeps track of floor votes, and organizes lots of small but important details of the work that the pages handle on the Senate floor. Since floor pages spend most of their time right in the middle of Senate sessions, they get a lot of visibility and more interaction with the Senate members.

Floor page jobs are awarded on the basis of a test – basically, to see how well you recognize individual senators, with their names and home states. My younger sister made up flash cards and we practiced until I was close to perfect.

I'm happy to say that I got the job. And from that point on, I was one of the pages who wasn't quite so invisible.

Of course, being visible is sometimes a mixed blessing. During one long afternoon session of the Senate I was sitting up on the rostrum, waiting to handle any urgent errand that might come up. I was tired, kind of bored, and trying hard to stay awake. That's when C-SPAN – the official Congressional television service – caught me nodding off during a broadcast sweep of the Senate floor that went out over national TV. And if that wasn't embarrassing enough, my parents called to say that they'd seen my moment of glory on C-SPAN. They still love to show that film clip to their friends.

Marielle Rabins
Weston, MA

"100% different from school"

I spent two years at the Southern Alberta Institute of Technology, studying to be an automotive technician. My instructors were great people, each with 25 to 30 years of industry experience. We spent five hours a day learning about technology and another two hours in the shop. By the time I got my diploma, I felt really knowledgeable about engines.

Then I started to look for a job. Oops. The ton of knowledge I'd acquired at school didn't seem to be what employers were looking for.

I did manage to find a part-time gig at a local Ford dealership. I worked the night shift, mostly cleaning floors. I was determined to work my way up to a real job as a technician, so I spent almost a year at Ford, hoping something would open up.

Finally, I got a call from a small Audi shop. They offered me a real job as a technician!

I started as an apprentice in this shop, but I expected that. It's standard industry practice for junior techs to spend at least two years as an apprentice under a more experienced journeyman. The journeyman is essentially a mentor — someone who teaches and watches over less experienced workers. In return, an apprentice is expected to drop everything and do whatever the journeyman asks. That usually meant all the dirty and boring work.

What did surprise me, however, was how little my two years of school had prepared me for a real job. School was mostly about theory — how things worked, how you measure engine performance and troubleshoot problems.

Working at Audi was 100% different from school. Theory wasn't important: an Audi technician's job is simply to figure out what's broken and fix it, usually by installing a new part. That's harder than it sounds: if you do a job wrong, it reflects badly on the whole shop and can cost a ton of money to fix right.

I learned quickly not to make the same mistake twice.

School also didn't prepare me for the pressure of working fast. The first engine I rebuilt took me 67 hours to finish. Now that I know what I'm doing, that same job will take just nine hours. Since the shop generally charges a flat rate for each job, technicians who work fast bring in more profits and are better paid. The rule here is, "Get it right, but don't take forever."

Something else that caught me by surprise was how closely everyone at Audi worked together. If you get really stuck, you ask someone and they help. We're like a family. We all talk to each other, and our boss is a guy I can always ask for advice.

At the same time, there's much more hierarchy than I expected at our shop. In school, I was part of a class of 30 or so people who were pretty much at the same level in terms of knowledge and experience. At Audi, the senior techs have tremendous experience, and there's a kind of etiquette about how a new apprentice like me would show respect for this experience. It wasn't an easy transition from school, but I've learned a lot about paying and earning respect.

Of course, school did teach a few lessons that were priceless in my real-world job. At SAIT, showing up on time was a big deal. Classroom doors were closed and locked at 8:00 in the morning, and if you were late or absent more than three times, you'd get kicked out school. By the time you earned a diploma, you'd certainly learned something about the work ethic!

Richard Twiddy
Calgary, Alberta

"A complete know-it-all"

I landed my first paying editorial job on a startup magazine called *The New Englander: A Journal of Business and Public Affairs* (yes, a ridiculously pretentious name that became *New England Business*). I was an assistant editor, hired mostly to do proofreading, copy-editing, and caption-writing. I couldn't even say I'd achieved a financial upgrade from my college waitressing gig. When I told my father about the new job, he observed that a 20% raise would barely get me to minimum wage.

However, being the most junior member of the magazine's staff didn't stop me from showing that I was a complete know-it-all. And not much of a team player, either.

I didn't waste a moment trying to grasp the political lay of the land. Instead, I made a couple of friends who encouraged my driving need to take charge and set everything straight. One of these friends was my direct supervisor, the managing editor. We started spending leisurely lunch hours dissecting the ill-conceived magazine that employed us. It was summer in New Hampshire, after all, and the magazine was a monthly. We could have probably gone to Europe and no one would have noticed our absence.

My second friend was a semi-retired sales guy who helped me understand how poorly our magazine was positioned for its market. Our young editor-in-chief wanted to write about "public affairs" and had zero interest in business; meanwhile, our ad sales people lusted after the low-hanging fruit of big corporate ad budgets. To make matters worse, my friend pointed out, our ad rates were so high that we found ourselves competing with *The Wall Street Journal* and other national publications. We didn't win those shoot-outs very often.

A wiser new employee would have kept her head down below her desk and, after a suitable apprenticeship, begun issuing diplomatic and tentative suggestions. Instead, before people even knew my name, the managing editor and I charged into the publisher's office, announcing that the company should fire the staff, move the publication to Boston (from rural New Hampshire), rename it, and — *ta-da!* — appoint me as the new editor.

Probably the only reason I wasn't fired on the spot was because the magazine was hemorrhaging money. Why the owners hadn't listened to their ad sales staff; why they hired a young, green editor and then another, greener one; why they couldn't fathom that a business magazine would fare better in an urban area where there were… uh, *businesses?* I have no clue.

Whatever the reason, the upshot was that we — the managing editor and I — were actually taken seriously. The publisher put us in charge of a complete top-down makeover of our magazine. With a warning: "You are going out on a limb, and if this doesn't work, we'll cut off the branch." I worked day and night to save that limb, and eventually watched the whole tree catch fire.

The magazine's frequency was increased to twice monthly — our suggestion, to make it more "timely." Doubling the number of issues with fewer staff, on a lean budget, without the resources of the parent company (we'd moved to Boston, as threatened)… all of these changes took a toll on quality. Typographical errors, thin reporting, blunders in judgment and content, everything that went wrong ended up on my desk, with my own name emblazoned at the top of the staff page.

Friendships were battered, too. The managing editor didn't like living in Boston; he resigned after six months and moved back to New Hampshire. The semi-retired sales guy, his dream fulfilled, retired to coastal Massachusetts — which might have been the moon for all I saw of him.

The rest of the staff returned my Christmas cards unopened.

Most poignantly, I realized that I *hated* business publishing, with its narrow scope and self-serving stories and inevitable incestuous relationships between advertisers and editorial. Was this why I had attended journalism school? To produce yet another article lauding the insurance industry, or preside at yet another rubber-chicken dinner honoring some flatulent CEO?

I did make it for two years, after which the company gave me a bonus check and a farewell luncheon. Management and a few of the surviving staff no doubt had a hell of a party after the door slammed behind me.

Therese Reger
Montreal, Quebec

"I have some notes to be typed"

While I was in grad school working on a Masters degree in music, I took a part-time clerical job at a major insurance company to fund my living expenses. I put in time as a receptionist, ran errands, filed reams of paper, and gradually learned the ins and outs of the insurance business.

I still needed a day job after graduation, but it didn't take me long to realize that the company where I'd been working simply would not promote anyone who had started as a part-time receptionist to their so-called "professional track," regardless of how smart they were or hard they worked. So I applied for an entry-level broker position at another firm — and they hired me! I was thrilled.

My co-workers in the clerical pool at my old company understood what a big deal this was. As a parting gift, they gave me a coffee cup with "Congratulations – You Made It!" written on one side and a picture of a dog resting his chin on the final rung of a stairway, looking at a big bone with a red ribbon, on the other side. From now on, I would get some respect. The secretary assigned to my new department would type *my* letters and file *my* paperwork!

The first day at my new job was great. My colleagues were welcoming, the work was interesting, and I felt valued. I stuck around a while after 5:00pm to set up my cubicle... and then my boss, an executive vice president, called me into his office. He and Fred, the firm's senior partner, had papers spread all over his desk. "Fred and I just got back from a meeting and I have some notes that really need to be typed up before Sally gets here tomorrow morning," my boss told me. "You can do this for us, right? It shouldn't take more than 15 minutes or so."

I was taken totally by surprise. My head was spinning, and all I could think of was that any answer I gave could have a big impact on my career. I finally nodded, said "Okay, sure," and took the notes to my boss's secretary's desk. I began typing – a job I knew only too well – meanwhile telling myself to stay calm so I could type those damn notes quickly and correctly, then get the **&#!! out of there. Trying to look composed, I delivered the typed notes to my boss and then fled the scene.

Once out of the building, the tears started. My cheeks were flushed and my heart was still racing. Here I was, back typing, and on my first day, no less! Should I have stood my ground and risked seeming petty or uncooperative? Would my boss take advantage of me or think less of me because I agreed to do clerical work? Was this an intentional test? If so, had I passed or failed? I realized that if I hadn't been there, my boss would have waited until his secretary came in the next morning. I saw his request as a form of manipulation; intentional or not, I couldn't say. My anger grew with each minute of the commute home.

I was living with my boyfriend at the time, an intelligent guy seven years older than me, who worked in education and social services. When I came through the door he asked how my first day had gone. The tears and anger rose up again as I told my story. "So what are you going to do about it?" he asked. I said I wasn't sure but my inclination was to confront my boss first thing the next day. I'd ask him why I was asked to do typing, and I'd remind him that multiple interviewers at the firm had told me that my job was supposed to be a professional position.

However, I had some doubts about this approach. Would I seem uncooperative, inflexible, or, worse yet, a pushy woman? I'll never forget my boyfriend's response: "You have to address this right away. Just say that you weren't hired to type and ask what to expect going forward. Whatever he says, it's your decision to stay or not; you're in control. Plus, they didn't spend all that time hiring what they thought was the best candidate to lose you over something like this. And in the unlikely event he says to pound sand on the typing thing, you'll have another job soon enough because you've got what it takes."

Of course, I knew he was right.

I went in the next day, gave my prepared speech as firmly and calmly as possible (admittedly with some butterflies in my stomach) and waited for my boss's reaction. With what almost seemed a Cheshire Cat grin he said, "Yeah, I guess you're right. I probably shouldn't have asked you. I won't do it again, okay?"

It wasn't a profuse apology, but it was enough for me to move forward. He was good to his word for the next six (very enjoyable) years I worked with him. He also became one of my most important mentors in the years to come. Ironically, there were times when I did some of my own typing, without resentment. It was just part of getting the job done, usually after hours when our secretary was gone and a deadline was bearing down on me. The key was that I did it on my own terms.

Carol McKeen
Waltham, MA

"Communicating with aliens"

When my fiance Michael and I and our dog Rusty arrived in Boulder, Colorado, we were wildly optimistic about our new life... but also very broke. We survived on a lot of rice, macaroni, and tuna fish. (Actually, Rusty usually ate better than we did.)

Michael managed to find a job waiting tables at a fine dining restaurant, but that didn't help our finances much. Michael decided to spend his earnings *plus* advances from our new infinite credit card line on computer hard drives for his latest entrepreneurial venture, building custom PCs. Meanwhile, I was furiously seeking any gig that read "Bachelor's Degree Preferred" in the job description.

Finally, I asked my cousin — who managed several businesses for clients — to help me find work.

My cousin did in fact know about a job opening in nearby Denver. The next day, I drove to an eerie-looking industrial area near Pecos and I-36 — no place a good-looking, 20-something young woman should have to visit — and found myself at the entrance to a gigantic recycled plastics factory. The sound was deafening as I made my way in and looked for my cousin and my new boss, a middle-aged guy named Charlie. Dozens of male workers stared at me and I smiled and waved. "This isn't why I went to college," I said to myself. "I busted my ass so I *wouldn't* end up working in a factory. I'm an English major!"

My cousin and Charlie met me in an upstairs office. I looked around at the hundreds of piles of paper, file folders, and trash that covered this filthy, plastic-scented room. To the right side of the door was another room with the old wooden door open halfway. I glanced inside and saw a giant TV and a bed, but then I was distracted by an enormous desktop PC that was sitting with a pile of software, all fresh out of the box.

"Welcome to CharCo," my cousin said and I introduced myself meekly. Then he said, "Here are about ten thousand files from 1976 and your job is to set up this PC and figure out how to make a database. Cool?" My cousin always tagged his ideas with "cool?" so without thinking I agreed. It quickly dawned on me why my cousin had said it would be fine to wear jeans and a t-shirt to work. This grubby room was my new office. This was going to be my new life. This was also the last day of my youth, the end of 22 years of freedom. Gone forever.

I spent a week with a vacuum cleaner and bottles of organic spider killer—the worst investment I'd ever made besides Michael's unprofitable PC-building business. Then, despite a near-total lack of experience with computers, I set up the PC, pored over the gigantic manuals, and began to learn MS Office and Access.

I was good, too. I went from setting up a database to learning how the recycling industry worked. I took charge of marketing, sales collateral, and print design, and Charlie's business began to attract more investors and clients. Although this wasn't my dream job, I realized that this was the way the world worked. Or at least this was the way I was living in the world.

I also became good friends with the lead foreman, Steve, who came to see me in my clean but maddeningly loud office at least twice daily, and he always had something to show me that was never boring or simple—in a mechanical sense, anyway. Steve also didn't hesitate to say he thought Charlie was both insane and clueless. "He has no idea how to run this place and he'd be out at least a million dollars in plastics machinery and accessories if it weren't for me," he muttered.

From Steve and others I heard that Charlie had inherited a few million dollars and purchased the factory not to save the world or repurpose discarded tires and fences and parking stops. No, Charlie bought the factory for another reason: He was constructing an enormous pod-like communication device so he could communicate with aliens. Or "Friends," as he called them.

After I'd been working at the company for a couple of months, Charlie trusted me enough to actually show me the Big Secret. Although I'd already heard a little about his project, he explained that this was a work still in progress, and he told me how he slept here and was up most nights crafting it and doing research. The UFO club that he and his wife attended in secret small towns every year had fueled Charlie's lifelong obsession. He loaned me a book on how the Bible was a direct correlation between the fact that we were born from an alien race and he, by god, knew it and was going to prove it with the help of his inheritance and insane genius.

What could I say? Welcome to the real world. It's bigger than you can know right now, kid.

Of course, I knew that Charlie was crazy. I could also see that he was rapidly losing touch with the reality of the recycling business. At this point my foreman friend Steve and I were running the company, while my cousin took charge of Charlie's other businesses. Finally there were the inevitable money and trust issues, and we were all laid off (excluding Steve who had a heart attack at age 28 shortly thereafter and later started his own business in retail).

Ironically, working at Charlie's insane company turned out to be a great career experience. I went on to become the "whiz kid" at a design firm, very appreciative of the knowledge I'd absorbed by learning how to set up a computer and network and database system. From here I moved on to various other jobs, including gigs as a Web analyst and as a professional musician and promoter. I've learned not to worry about big life transitions — they're just an opportunity to learn and grow some more.

Wendy Clark
Denver, CO

"I wrote my own job description"

While I was in college, I spent my summers working for a company in Burlington, Vermont that was the major distributor of newspapers, magazines and books in the northern part of the state. I had what amounted to a paper route—I got up early, loaded up my truck and delivered boxes of publications to bookstores, drug stores and convenience stores throughout a 60-mile territory on the east side of Burlington (sometimes interrupted by a quick swim on a really hot day).

It was a fun job, but as graduation time crept closer I began to worry about what I was going to do once I left school. I heard lots of advice from family, friends, coaches, and professors, and I attended job fairs and went on interviews... but nothing really clicked.

Then during spring break of my senior year I ran into my old boss from the Burlington distribution company. He told me about a new division he wanted to launch, helping three local colleges manage their textbook ordering. Would I be interested in coming on board as the textbook sales manager?

"Absolutely!" I said. I suddenly realized that all the other jobs I'd explored were missing one critical element: the energy and urgency of a startup. What I really wanted was to help build something new and important. And here it was.

We talked about the details all through the rest of my spring semester. The new company had to be up and running in time for the start of the coming academic year, which meant an early August launch date. I reported for work in mid-May, almost before the ink on my diploma had dried. And from that point on it was a sprint for both of us.

I quickly learned an important lesson about working for a startup: job descriptions change constantly. When my new boss described my role during our spring meeting, he said I'd be responsible for understanding how each college client handled textbook orders, and then for learning how each publisher processed those orders. Then I'd have to come up with a plan for how we'd connect both ends with our own systems for ordering, distribution, inventory management, and returns. As I explored the market, I wrote up my own job description to make sure I didn't miss any critical steps.

But once we had our systems in place, the job shifted from theory to real life. Now it was my responsibility to make sure orders were submitted on time (which meant pushing the college staff to get textbook decisions and orders from faculty members in a timely way—a major headache). I had to make sure the books we ordered were received and documented. I kept track of all of our inventory and placed endless numbers of special orders. And then when books didn't sell, I had to process returns and set up credits that would be applied toward next semester's orders. Oh, and I was also the guy who met with the sales reps from individual textbook companies (which gave me a real education in what a truly creative expense account looks like).

These new responsibilities put a heavy focus on being organized—meticulously organized, in fact. I had to stay on top of people who were supposed to meet deadlines, I had to troubleshoot when orders didn't arrive, and I had to make quick updates when book orders were changed at the last minute. Again, it was important to stay on top of all the details, so I wrote a brand-new job description for myself and kept adding to it as new issues popped up.

I also learned another important lesson: In a startup, your boss is going to give you constant feedback on your performance. Forget about annual reviews or that occasional chat with the boss. I got constant feedback about what I was doing, with frequent course corrections as the needs of the business changed. This wasn't micro-management—instead, my boss and I had an ongoing conversation about our priorities and the kind of support I'd need as my job evolved. I understood that the business literally wouldn't succeed if I shifted my focus from essential tasks to things that were less important.

The summer was hectic, but by our August launch date we were processing textbook orders for our three client colleges with barely a glitch. The startup sprint had been successful, so once again my job description changed... but every day continued to be an adventure, and I loved every minute of it.

Mark Flanagan
Sudbury, MA

"Two patients"

All through high school, I dreamed about a career in nursing. In college, I worked steadily on a four-year plan that would lead eventually to admission to an elite nursing program at UCLA, one of the best in California. My Armenian grandmother didn't quite understand how many years it would take for me to get my RN license; she immediately began bragging to her friends about my wonderful career.

Finally, I hit the jackpot—an internship at a hospital in Los Angeles. I was convinced that working with real nurses and therapists would give me the edge I needed to get into the UCLA program I wanted.

It only took me a month to realize what all my planning and studying was leading to: a life of little more than stress, time management, and charting. Endless charting. For a few weeks, I told myself it would be worth it if I could make a difference in the lives of patients. After all, I told myself, all jobs have their downsides.

Then I met my first patient. I was helping a nurse with an elderly man who had taken part in some military action while in the U.S. Air Force. At some point he'd lost his ability to speak so I nodded along as he gestured and made guttural noises, showing me how planes flew high and then dove low to drop bombs or release soldiers on parachutes. At least, that's what I thought he was saying. *He* knew what he was trying to say, of course, but it all came out as gibberish. He had an Air Force pin that I fastened to his gown every time I changed him and a matching cap that he kept adjusting over his puffs of white hair. He was my patient for over a month and then he was released.

A week later, I overheard another intern talking about a man who had been admitted to the emergency room the night before. He hadn't lived, she said, and she added that the man had an Air Force pin fastened to his shirt. I checked, and yes, he was the same patient I'd spent a month helping.

I'd lost my first patient... but it felt like I'd lost a good friend. All the stress of dealing with other sometimes-difficult patients, the weeks of high pressure exams, nights I spent studying rather than sleeping, and the constant obsession with working toward my RN license—why was I doing this? I asked myself. Worse, I could see that the job wouldn't get any better once I became a fully qualified nurse. I saw the hours that the nurses spent updating charts rather than speaking with patients, and the constant threat of legal action that surrounded hospital workers like a maze of swords.

Sure, I'd made a difference in one man's life while he was my patient. But then he died and that just wasn't enough for me any more.

I'd already run up $5,000 in school debt and was only halfway to a diploma—and I was abandoning a career I hadn't even started. With no idea what I was doing and feeling a growing sense of panic, I had a hard time even leaving my bed in the mornings. My grades slipped and I took fewer and fewer shifts at the hospital. I lost a bunch of weight very fast and I wasn't sleeping. It was terrifying, thinking that I was stuck in a career I hated.

Then I met my second patient.

I was leaving work one day when a new patient waved me into her room. She had been admitted at the same time as I was signing out. I was exhausted and ready to faint from hunger, but I walked into her room and introduced myself as an intern. Was there anything I could do for her? I asked. Instead of answering, she just shook her head and pointed at her ears. I realized that she couldn't hear me. She mimed brushing her teeth and I realized that she just wanted a toothbrush.

As it happened, I'd learned a little American Sign Language four years ago, in high school. In broken ASL, I greeted her and introduced myself again. I told her I knew the basics of ASL and she looked so relieved, so relaxed at finally having someone who could communicate with her. I learned that she was waiting for the hospital's ASL interpreter to show up, so I sat with her for an hour after my shift, signing with her and keeping her calm. She was extremely patient with my poor ASL skills. We slowly exchanged stories and she told me how she felt like she was in a foreign country with everyone talking *around* her and not *to* her.

When I finally left the hospital, I remember feeling relaxed and calm myself. That evening I announced to a room full of relatives that I was going to become a Deaf Studies major, that I wanted to be an interpreter so I could breach the gap between deaf people and hearing people. The first response I got was booming laughter from my uncle.

"You're going to work with deaf and mute people?" he asked me, gesturing wildly and cracking up. He didn't understand the difference between interpreting, taking one language into your brain and spitting another out, and translating, or taking written language and rewriting it in a different language at your own leisure. My grandma, who had proudly announced that she had a "nurse granddaughter" to every grocery store clerk, was reduced to blubbering sobs. She no longer talked about my career choice. My mom didn't say anything.

I spent the next week running around school from one department to another, asking permission to change my major and throwing out my four-year plan for a new plan. It was too late to start a new major from the beginning, so my advisor told me to skip the first language class and jump right into American Sign Language 2.

The first month of school was really hard. I didn't understand the professor in my advanced ASL class and, like the deaf lady in the hospital, I felt like I was alone in a foreign country when I sat in class. But I refused to give up because I had finally found where I belonged. The culture, the language, I fell in love with it. I studied for hours a day, between classes and before bed. I went to many different gatherings of deaf people around Los Angeles and absorbed the language and adjusted my behavior to match their cultural norms. By the end of the semester, my classmates complimented me on how fast I signed and how natural my facial expressions seemed. They acted like I was just gifted rather than disciplined, calling me "lucky."

I also took summer classes to catch up and found a minimum wage job to avoid more loans. Now, I work part-time and study full-time at my school, which didn't offer a nursing major for students earning their first degree, but is one of the best schools and communities for Deaf Studies. Connecting with my second patient made all the difference in my life: With her inspiration, I landed right where I needed to be all along.

Cynthia Ghazary
Burbank, CA

"Christmas in July"

My first actual paying job was as a part-time banquet server at the Commonwealth Club, an elegant "gentlemen's club" in downtown Richmond, VA. The pay was great, the hours didn't interfere with my college schedule, and the members seemed to be mostly fun, laid-back people. (Did I mention that the pay was great?)

Then one day the Club picked up a large off-site catering assignment that changed my whole perspective.

Some notable, wealthy Virginia-bred man and an equally noteworthy woman were getting married at a historic plantation on a beautiful day in July. Nothing new except that the family was going to supply their own liquor. That meant all the banquet servers were going to act up because we were offsite, and our managers weren't going to be counting the liquor bottles. The whole crew was in a light-hearted, happy mood.

By this time, I'd been made an unofficial manager myself, so the crew's enthusiasm for this job was good news. Maybe, just maybe, I wouldn't have to work as hard at the end of the night to rally the troops to finish the last leg. Catering jobs are hard work given that we have to set up literally *everything*, from our workspace in the back to the front of the house where the guests ooh and aah over gold-rimmed charger plates.

I liked being in charge of this kind of big project, and I always felt it was imperative to stay on top of what needed to be done, keep a smile on my face and not let the small stuff break me. I also loved how the other servers listened to me and respected me and the way my managers gave me free license to direct our staff when needed.

The ceremony and the cocktail hour went along smoothly, and then we arrived at one of my favorite parts of the work shift — the table assignments. The banquet crew doesn't get many moments where an individual server is recognized as a superstar, so being assigned to the head table or one close to it (where the parents, grandparents, and other important wedding party members sit) is the closest you get to an attaboy in this job.

Naturally, I was pleased to be given the head table. But I soon discovered that the groom was a complete and total pompous jerk (and that's not the word I used in my head). This wasn't just typical waitress complaining about a bad customer: The groom grabbed my arm to let me know I didn't top off his water, pulled my jacket because he ran out of butter, and snapped his fingers in my face to let me know he'd finished his meal. I thought I'd reached my limit... and then he tripped me, stepped on my leg as he stumbled, and then walked away as if I was some sort of inanimate object he'd caught his foot on. His new wife leaned over me and scrunched up her face to ask if I was okay, and my response was "Yes, but are you?" She frowned, quickly put on a stiff smile, then walked away too. I didn't see her the rest of the night.

After cake was served neither the bride nor groom came back to their table. My good friend, who had the table next to me, winked and then walked off. That was the Commonwealth Club signal for "it's time to have fun." I followed my friend over to a secluded area in the gardens to where the barbacks were breaking down bars and rearranging bottles.

At that moment I looked back at the banquet area and saw the groom laughing. I felt a rush of raw anger. I realized that the groom had no concept of how much his rudeness had hurt my self-respect. One of the barbacks looked at me and said, "Yeah, I know that guy's a real ***. Just go ahead and take something from the bar. He won't know." I tried to give the same speech I always do about how we shouldn't drink on the job, how it's stealing and we're better than that. The barback cut me off and said, "But it's Christmas in July. There's no way to tell what we take, all of those people are drunk. Plus, let's be real. You're not getting a tip. Not from him. You deserve some payback for how hard you work."

I looked at him for a minute, nodded my head, then reached for a bottle of Champagne. For the first time in my working life I drank on the job. To be precise, I drank some imported Russian bubbly from a very old $150 bottle of Cristal. And because I was taking it from the notable, wealthy Virginia-bred man who had no manners, I felt good about it. Really good. So good that about half the bottle quickly vanished.

And then I remembered it was "rallying the troops" time. Feeling a bit tipsy, I went back to work.

Nothing crazy happened while we were breaking down, but at some point my manager must have noticed something since he asked me to go to the company van, saying I had done enough. I pulled him aside and asked him what that meant. He said he knew that the groom was a jerk and that it was a long day but if anyone could handle it he thought it would be me. And if there was an issue I should have come to him about it. This made me even angrier but I said nothing and just went to sit in the van. Before the night was over I had come to the conclusion that the only thing I liked about this job was the pay.

Over the next few days, I realized that my manager had been absolutely right to be disappointed. I was disappointed myself. I'd gotten mad, let my integrity go and for the first time ever I disgraced myself on the job. The only real highlight of that workday for me was drinking really expensive champagne as a form of petty protest.

Even worse, I knew I'd probably act exactly the same way if I had a second chance. I think that's what got to me. What was the point of doing this job except for the money? I wasn't helping people. I didn't make a difference or challenge myself in any way. These things meant something to me, they inspired me. They made it possible for me to carry myself with dignity and be an example so that I can receive respect and motivate others. If I couldn't hang on to my self-respect in a catering job, then I had to move on.

Shortly afterwards, I went to my manager at the Commonwealth Club and said, "I quit."

Whitney Shepperson
Richmond, VA

"Beard Employment"

At a paint store around the corner
from where I did abide,
I saw a Help Wanted sign
and so I went inside.

Behind the counter stood a man
with a beard down to his waist.
I asked him for an application
and he gave me one post haste.

I filled it out completely
as neatly as I could.
I gave it to the bearded man
and then he said, "You should

Come back again tomorrow"
as he stroked his hairy chin.
"I'll give this to the boss man
the moment he comes in."

"What time should I arrive?" I asked.
"Make it half past two,
And I suggest you do not shave,
if you know what's good for you."

I returned the following day
promptly at half past two.
The bearded man, he greeted me,
"The Boss man will see you."

I followed him between the aisles
to the rear of the store.
He said, "I see you did not shave."
as he knocked upon the door.

"Enter," said a friendly voice.
And so I went inside.
Before me sat the Boss man
with a beard both long and wide.

I thought they must be brothers,
the men who run this store.
I had never seen two men
with such long beards before.

"So, you want to work for me?"
"Yes, sir" I replied.
He looked at the application...
"Hmm...But are you qualified?

Step a little closer
I need to see your chin.
Ah, I see you did not shave.
I think you will fit in.

The job requires mixing paint
and stocking all the shelves.
And most important, employees
must all improve themselves."

"Improve themselves? What do you mean?
I don't understand."
"If you're going to work for me
there's one thing I demand.

You can never cut, or trim,
or shave your beard again.
All of my employees become
mega bearded men!"

"I can grow a beard," I said,

157

"I've had one before."
"To work here you'll need to grow
your beard down to the floor.

Full natural long beards
aren't for the faint of heart.
I'll teach you to embrace them
as a manly work of art.

The starting rate is eight per hour.
That is what it pays.
But for every inch of beard you grow
You'll earn an extra raise.

Once a month all beards are measured.
I keep a written chart..."
"You'll pay me to grow my beard?
All right! When can I start?"

"Come in Monday morning.
We open up at nine.
From now on no more shaving."
"Okay, by me, that's fine!"

And so I started Monday
with stubble on my face.
The other guys had awesome beards
and I felt out of place.

"We all started out like you,
once upon a time,
but if you never cut your beard
then it will grow sublime,"

Said the assistant manager,
the waist-length bearded, Joe.
He had worked there for three years
And man did his beard grow!

The twins, Ben and Andy,
had beards down past their chest.
They competed with each other

to see whose beard was best.

The Boss Man's beard was past his knees,
thick and so impressive.
He always said, "It's way too short.
It needs to grow excessive!"

I started in the stock room
while my beard was short and scruffy.
I got to wait on customers
once my beard grew nice and fluffy.

I learned how to give discounts
to men who did not shave.
The longer a man's beard was
the more he got to save.

Words of beard encouragement
were posted here and there,
reminding us and customers
to grow our facial hair.

On the last day of each month
the Boss man he would measure
our beards, from chin to tip,
The results gave us such pleasure.

We would go and celebrate.
The boss would buy us beers.
His words of encouragement
were music to our ears.

He would give us pep talks
about why beards were good
not only for the business
but for manly brotherhood.

Our beards were the store's branding.
They set our store apart
from the competition.
The concept was quite smart.

Our beards were advertising.
In town we were well known
not just for our paint products
but for the beards we had grown.

I stayed on for three short years
'til I had to move out West.
By the time I left the paint store
my beard covered my chest.

I am grateful for that paint store
and their Beard Employment quirk.
For now I am an actor
who gets lots of bearded work.

Kai Cofer
Northridge, CA

"Bonded forever"

I'd spent a year or so meandering around Europe, doing odd jobs and writing English-language lyrics for musicians. I finally ended up in Athens on a drizzly, cold Sunday, having dinner with my friend Mandy's Greek family. "Is this what Greek weather is like?" I asked. "I was hoping for a little more sun."

"Why don't you take a job on a cruise ship?" Mandy's father asked. "They'll take you to warmer places."

"Oh sure, " I said. "A cruise line is just waiting to hire me!"

"Well, let me make a call..."

Sure enough, Mandy's father knew someone high up in a cruise ship line. I quickly pulled together a resume and the next morning he drove me down to the port of Piraeus, where several gleaming cruise ships were berthed. We walked into a building with several floors of seemingly frantic people doing all sorts of things with a great sense of urgency. As we walked through the third floor offices I noticed that people stared at me with great

160

suspicion. And then I was introduced to the port captain of the cruise line.

Captain Ferentinos was in charge of the engineering side of operations, which included selecting officers for the three cruise ships that belonged to the family-owned fleet. The captain's imposing, take-charge manner made him a force to be reckoned with. He started by asking me a few questions about my background. I had interned at a radio station over the summers during college and had occasionally helped in my father's general contracting business, but I had no real professional work history. As I tried my best to create a reason to be hired with such limited experience, I realized it was time to start considering finding a stable job if I was going to get anywhere in life. I was 24 years old.

After a few more questions, he told me that he wanted me to meet the owner of the cruise line and escorted me down the corridor to a corner office. All eyes seemed to be on me and I imagined myself meeting someone who would resemble Aristotle Onassis. I waited by the door for a few moments and then the captain took me into the owner's office. There, behind a massive desk, sat a woman with large glasses. She looked up and over a pile of papers as I shook her hand and introduced myself and handed her my resume.

She glanced at it for a moment and suddenly with great enthusiasm said, "You're Hungarian! My grandmother was Hungarian and my fondest memories of my childhood were with her." She motioned me to sit down and quickly dismissed Captain Ferentinos, who now suddenly seemed to be an intruder as opposed to her protector.

Imagine Meryl Streep's character in "The Devil Wears Prada" and throw in an Italian accent and more jewelry. This was my new boss. I learned two things within that ten-minute exchange that changed my life and career. First, everyone was terrified of her and second, she had a last name that very few people could pronounce.

She hired me on the spot and told me I would be working on board her flagship as the secretary to the captain and the cruise director. She told me I would begin training the following day in the office and should come in for the remainder of the week. The following Monday I would board the ship and sail through the Mediterranean and Europe before crossing the ocean to spend the winter in the Caribbean and on the Amazon.

When I arrived for my first day at the office (earlier than my appointed hour), I saw Captain Ferentinos and asked him to teach me how to pronounce the signora's last name (everybody addressed her as "Mrs. K" and I was determined to set myself apart from others.) After repeated mistakes, I finally got it right and was pleased by the look on her face when I addressed her by her full name.

Mrs. K was a demanding, detail-oriented, micromanaging type of boss and matriarch. I learned quickly that her husband had passed away only a few months earlier and she was left to run the business with her two sons, who were close to my age. I think my eagerness to be an excellent employee coupled with my ability to absorb information quickly (along with the Hungarian advantage) impressed her.

On the day I boarded the ship she was there overseeing everything. She told me my private cabin would be in officer's quarters right next to the captain. She displaced a woman who had been working for the cruise line for three years. This was the beginning of a lot of resentment directed toward me. Just prior to leaving on the first cruise of my life, I handed my new boss a thank you card for trusting me and giving me the opportunity to work for her and for having trust in me. I promised to work hard and prove that she had made the right decision.

I settled in quickly and realized how much there was to learn. About ten days later the ship docked in France and the energy of the vessel changed completely from calm and orderly to chaotic fear. The owner was coming on board! I was unfazed and within 20 minutes of her arrival I heard my name being paged to report to the Grill Bar. I had no idea what was up and when I came up the steps I found a long line of crew members waiting to speak with the owner about various things or to file their complaints. I had no clue why I had been summoned and took my place in line. When she saw me out of the corner of her eye, she yelled my name (she called me by my middle name, which is definitively Hungarian) and everyone else just stared at me. She asked me to sit down, ordered a coffee for me and then leaned in closely and said, "I just *knew* you would be marvelous at this. I have big plans for you. Now… tell me *everything*."

Six months later she took me off the ship and brought me to New York, where I would spend the winter season with her working as her assistant and then we would spend summers in Greece when the ship sailed the Mediterranean. I worked for her (tirelessly) for almost six years. She took me under her wing and taught me everything about superior hospitality, organization, excursion planning, marketing, itinerary planning, hiring, training and dealing with logistics and surprises. I wrote the brochures that made people want to explore the world and was paid handsomely for it.

That first Christmas without her husband the signora came on board the ship to travel. The crew was terrified. I sensed her loneliness. While the crew enjoyed a two-day break between cruises and went ashore to feel like landlubbers, I stayed behind and asked her if she needed anything. We ate dinner together in the dining room and then decorated the Christmas tree in the main lounge in silence until 2:00am. No words were exchanged about that event but it bonded us forever.

Patricia Smith
Santa Monica, CA

"Surrounded by Eskimos"

I'd just finished a graduate degree in Industrial Engineering and Operations Research, and the recruiters seemed to think I was a real catch. They were especially impressed by my thesis on computer modeling of production control, which was a state of the art technology at that time. I was ready to go to work and change the world!

One recruiter for a multi-billion dollar market leader was particularly persuasive. "This is an area of technology of great interest to us," I was told. "We really want to put these ideas into practice." That was exactly what I wanted to hear.

I showed up for work right after graduation. The HR department seemed well organized: They gave me a tour of the facilities, explained company policies, and showed me my new desk, chair, and office. Okay so far.

Then I met my new boss. He knew who I was, but not a whole lot else. In fact, everything the campus recruiting team had promised seemed to have evaporated. I had to educate my new boss about my background, what I had done, and — more importantly — what I wanted to do for the company.

My boss was sympathetic and promised to do his best. Until he could straighten out the problem, he said he had to use me somehow. At first, I was given some makeshift assignments and was asked to read a few manuals. I was ready to work hard, but I quickly got the impression that the office was a pretty chaotic place.

Then my boss came up with my first real assignment: I was given a stopwatch and sent off to do a simple time and motion study. I knew he meant well, but I was sorely disappointed by this turn of events. I felt like I'd taken off in a plane, hoping to land in sunny Hawaii, where I'd be surrounded by surfers... but instead I'd landed in Alaska, surrounded by Eskimos. The Eskimos were very nice people, but they were Eskimos and no amount of niceness was going to make them into surfers!

I didn't want to disappoint my new managers, so I completed my little time and motion study successfully and my boss said he was pleased with the results. But I didn't feel any better when he told me that I was doing a good job. It wasn't the job I'd been hired to do, and I wanted to move on to the kind of challenging work that I'd trained for.

However, this was my first job, and I wasn't sure how hard to push for a better assignment. I kept saying to myself that this was just a communication mishap — *my* problem, not anyone else's — and things would be fixed eventually. And I was the new kid on the block, so I felt I had to prove I could do real work successfully. It also didn't help that I came from a cultural background that basically says, "Thou shall respect and obey your parents, gurus, bosses, and older relatives."

I thought about leaving the company – but I needed the money to pay my bills. I wanted to ask someone in my department for advice, but I worried that any co-worker would immediately leak the news to my managers and I'd lose my job. I really felt trapped.

It took me a good six months of stress and unhappiness before I finally admitted to myself that the job just wasn't going to work out. In the end, it didn't take me long to find a new job that took advantage of my skills and desires (I spent almost ten years at this second job, incidentally).

Looking back, I wish somebody in my first company had just said something like, "There's been a mistake, and I don't think we can give you the kind of assignments our recruiter promised you." With the best of intentions, mistakes do happen. But no one wanted to take responsibility or admit that there was even a problem. That shouldn't have happened.

M. M. (Sath) Sathyanarayan
San Diego, CA

"Folding laundry"

The summer I turned 17, I finally decided to get a job. But job hunting in a small town is hard. I was still in high school, and it seemed that everywhere I applied was already fully-staffed or "just not hiring at this moment." Very frustrating.

Then I got lucky. I was hanging out in our local laundromat with a buddy who was busy washing his gym clothes, and the only seat I could find was next to a grumpy-looking old man. A few minutes later the old man began chatting with me, just small talk about how my day was going, and why I looked so stressed. I explained to him that I was under a lot of pressure from my parents to find a job and that I was having trouble doing so. He asked me what I was good at, what experience I had, and how much money I needed to make. These were all questions I hadn't even asked myself, so giving him a clear answer was harder than I expected. Finally he pointed at the laundromat's bulletin board. "Go have a look," he said.

There, staring me in the face, was a Help Wanted ad for an individual to assist with doing laundry.

"Hey, I can do laundry!" I said to myself. But then I looked more closely: the ad had no contact information.

I sat back down next to the elderly man and explained the problem. "Too bad," he said. "Guess you'll have to keep looking."

Just then my buddy came over and asked me to help fold his clean clothes (folding laundry is definitely not a male skill). I noticed a lady nearby who was folding what seemed like a mountain of sheets, and I asked her how she happened to have such a huge pile. She smiled at me and explained that she and a few other people did laundry for a nursing home and that her last employee had recently quit on her. "By any chance are you the person who placed the ad on the bulletin board over there?" I asked. She was, and a few minutes later I had the job!

The next day I showed up at the laundromat after class. Kathy, my new boss, was there with another helper named Douglas and the biggest stack of laundry bags I'd ever seen, all full of dirty clothes. We had to weigh the bags first (the total came to 714 pounds) and then fill the washers with all the clothes. It was the worst smell I could have ever imagined.

Douglas turned out to be one lazy guy. He walked around the laundromat aimlessly pretending to help other customers in the laundromat, and he would do anything to get out of folding clothes. Kathy eventually left us two to do everything alone because we had a handle on things, and she returned to her regular job.

As the weeks passed, I learned to mostly ignore Douglas, and I started to focus more on the people around me who were doing their own laundry. It was always interesting to step back and see the diversity of the customers. Most days I'd make small talk with people while working, and I started noticing a few regulars, who were often older people. I loved listening to their stories about how they used to pay five cents to wash clothes, or how back then they didn't have the luxury of washing clothes in machines at all. A lot of them also thought it was so great that we were washing the clothes of the elderly stuck in that nursing home.

A few months into the job, I began to notice a homeless man who came by pretty regularly, sometimes coherent, other times, belligerent. The homeless man's name was Niko, he had dirty gray hair, wore gray sweats, sunglasses, any baseball cap he could find, and a black leather trench coat. The laundromat owner was well aware of Niko, and I was told to call the police if Niko came in because the owner had banned him from the property.

Most days Niko would walk by outside, drunk and mumbling to himself, minding his own business. But other days were worse. One day it was raining heavily outside, and Niko had come inside for shelter. I didn't want to be evil, so I told him he could stay inside until the rain let up. He went to lie down on a bench near the vending machines, and I continued folding my clothes. Then a small child began to cry. Next thing I know, Niko was screaming "Shut the f*** up!" at the child! I immediately told him to leave, but instead he locked himself in the restroom. Even though the mother of the child spoke very little English, I was able to tell her that I'd call the police if Niko came near them again. A half hour later, smoke started coming from under the bathroom door and Niko walked out, smoking a cigar. I called the police and they took him away.

Niko wasn't the only homeless person who would seek shelter at the laundromat—but he was the only one who caused trouble. I met other homeless men and women: Some were alcoholics and some were just down on their luck. I made an effort to speak to them while other laundromat customers just scurried away. And speaking to these people opened my eyes to how serious the homeless issue is and how many of these people are just looking to be heard. I can't tell you how many times they told me they were usually treated as less than human, and how often they had tears in their eyes just because I paid attention to them or just asked how they were doing.

By the end of the summer, my career as a laundry specialist came to an end. But much to my surprise, washing and folding piles of dirty clothes had been an awesome, humbling learning experience. I will forever have a soft spot in my heart for the homeless population and I currently do a lot of volunteer work within my community. I also now work in health services, a career where I feel I can make a difference in people's lives, even just on a small scale. As simple and random a job as the laundry gig was, it was more life-changing than I could've ever imagined.

Jasmin Skinner
Denver, CO

"My co-workers were less than thrilled"

I've always been a huge hockey fan, for sure. So when I heard that the Calgary Flames were hiring part-time ushers, I thought that would be a pretty cool job. The schedule turned out to be tough—the ushers had to work whenever the team played, which was usually nights, weekends, and holidays. We also had to be available for big-ticket concerts, other sporting events, tournaments, ice shows, circuses, and conventions at the Saddledome. With this kind of pressure, there was always a lot of turnover among the ushers.

The turnover helped me move up through the ranks pretty fast. I'm the kind of person who steps up to the plate when a job needs to be done, so within a few months I was promoted to be an ushering supervisor, which is a second-level supervisor position over the head ushers and part-timers. This was still a part-time job, though. I asked if the team would be willing to make my job full-time, and they finally did.

Much to my surprise, the other ushers — my former co-workers — were less than thrilled by my rapid promotion. "Who do you think you are?" one of the head ushers said to me. "Some of us have been here ten or fifteen years, and we know a lot more than you do." Of course, these same critics had made it clear that they didn't *want* to be promoted. "Too much responsibility," they said. Now all of a sudden they didn't trust me. It was weird.

One of the things they complained about was that supervisors and other back-office staff didn't wear uniforms, just regular street clothes. This was a sports team, remember, where almost everyone felt it was cool to wear the same team colors as the players. But now my former co-workers thought I was putting on airs by *not* wearing a uniform.

I knew the griping would eventually blow over, and I was confident I could do my job well enough to win over the critics. I also had an incredible boss, the vice president of building operations, who had worked for the Saddledome and the Calgary Fairgrounds for 30 years. I knew I could count on her for advice and support.

Then I uncovered a problem that really shook me up.

The ushers I supervised also helped the team's marketing department with distributing prizes, promotions, gift cards, and other incentives. I'd been vaguely aware that some of the leftovers were occasionally given to the ushers — kind of a perk of the job. Nothing to get excited about.

But when I took a closer look, I realized that a whole bunch of our ushers were taking more than just unwanted "leftovers." They were pocketing items of real value... and sometimes even forging the names of the ticket buyers who were supposed to get these items.

"Oh dear, this is stealing," I said to myself.

What was the right way to handle this situation? Ignore the unethical behavior? Identify the culprits and make sure they lost their jobs? Whatever I did, I realized, would probably destroy the trust and friendship that I was trying to build with my team of ushers. In fact, I'd be lucky to hang on to my own job if the situation turned ugly.

After thinking about my options, I went to my boss and told her what was happening. She agreed that we had to take action. We then took our conclusions to the marketing department—after all, it was the marketing department's promotional items that were being stolen.

My boss and I had already decided that the real problem we faced was a *pattern of behavior*, not outright dishonesty. Previous supervisors had done nothing to stop petty pilfering, and most of the current ushers could reasonably say, "Everybody's doing it." That wasn't entirely true, but clearly many of the ushers thought their pilfering was just a big game. I felt that we should certainly punish deliberate dishonesty, but bad behavior was better handled by trying to *change* that behavior.

With this perspective in mind, we figured out a solution that was easy to implement. The marketing department created a new set of rules for handling promotional gifts: Ushers had to collect an actual piece of a customer's event program (with a winning number) to collect a promotional item or gift card. We kept much better records of every marketing campaign, so almost nothing was "left over" or "lost."

Almost instantly, the problem of theft stopped.

We also decided not to make a general announcement about what we were doing. The new rules came from the marketing department, not us. Nobody was fired or even reprimanded—though at least some of the ringleaders could read between the lines. They got the message.

And along the way, my once-skeptical co-workers began to show more respect and trust for me as their new boss.

Kelly Moran
Calgary, Alberta

"It wasn't the job I wanted"

There I was... on my last semester of college, about to graduate with a BA in video production with plans to go straight into Hollywood filmmaking. Just one hitch: I needed to complete some kind of internship before I could graduate. I must have sent out several hundred applications—and finally got a single response.

There wasn't much to like about the offer: I'd be working for a company that produced films for TV (not exactly Hollywood material), the internship was unpaid, and I'd have to commute from New Jersey to New York (a huge sacrifice on my student budget). But I didn't have much choice. And once I started working, I discovered that my duties mainly consisted of updating the company's YouTube channel and other mundane stuff, none of which had much to do with my real career plans.

So I was taken by surprise when my boss called me into his office a month before graduation and offered me a real, full-time, paying job (provided I got my diploma). The job would be as the company's Associate Producer of New Media. For a new graduate (heck, not even a graduate yet) in a terrible economy, this was an amazing opportunity.

But it wasn't the job I wanted. Producers don't usually do the hands-on creative work of filmmaking, and I was sure I'd hate the job I was being offered.

My boss could see I was ambivalent about the offer, and then he said the magic words: "Stick with me and by the time you leave this job, you'll have a reel that no one in your graduating class could match." I'd already seen the company's own demo reel, so I knew my boss's clients were some of the biggest names you could think of. Name any record labels, actors, musicians, or movie studios, and my boss had worked with them. I was sold.

The first few months on the job were slow—just a few interviews and satellite media tours—and I was beginning to wonder if I'd made a mistake. Then my new company landed a big gig: a documentary that would accompany a special release of an upcoming concert in New York's Central Park. I got even more excited when I learned that the singer was Andrea Bocelli, one of the best and most renowned tenors and proponents of classical music. Bocelli has been blind nearly all his life and his voice is often said to be like velvet and thunder. Being involved with *this* production was a big, big deal.

We started work on the Bocelli documentary in August, and I got my first true taste of what being a producer was like. I went to giant production meetings, made a million phone calls, secured crews, location permits, equipment, you name it. Every day was very hectic and full of adrenaline.

I also discovered that my boss could get incredibly nasty and mean. At some early point in the production, someone made a mistake. My boss sent a scathing email to the entire crew, full of capital letters and exclamation marks. One of his sentences actually looked like he punched the keyboard ten times.

I found myself occasionally on the receiving end of lots of verbal abuse and email blasts. My boss wasn't exactly a helpful guy, either. One night I'd been working late at the concert site in Central Park and didn't have a way to get back home to New Jersey. I ended up sleeping in a run-down production trailer that had no heating and nothing to lay down on except the filthy floor. My boss came by the next day and let me go home... but he warned me that I had to return to work no later than 6:00pm. That's the kindest he was for the remainder of that project.

By the time we completed our end of the Bocelli project, I had amassed dozens of terrible emails. It got to a point that whenever my phone received a email notification, I would briefly panic and hoped it wasn't my boss. It was as if I had PTSD—any incoming email would send me into a panic. Did I really want a career in an industry that treated people this badly?

Before walking out the door, however, I decided to do some long-overdue research into television careers. I found an incredible memoir by Wendy Walker, a veteran CNN producer who had spent 30 years in television. Walker wrote about how she met presidents, religious leaders, best-selling authors, and of course Larry King, whose *Larry King Live* show she managed as executive producer. All her ups and downs, people she met, cool projects while working around the world, and much more. She witnessed history happen first-hand many times.

I kept talking to other people about careers in TV production, but Walker's story made all the difference. I learned that the chaotic environment that a producer deals with constantly is not something just anyone can survive. I realized that being successful in this environment takes a certain kind of temperament... and I had that temperament. I promised myself that I would keep working for my boss no matter how bad it got. I even promised myself that I'd eventually work at CNN, just like Wendy Walker.

So I spent another two-plus years working for my boss, learning to be a competent TV producer. The job never got easier, and my boss never became less unpleasant toward his employees. My nasty email collection kept growing exponentially, but I also got to work with Beyonce, Bon Jovi, Disney, Dreamworks, Universal, Def Leppard, and others. It seemed like a fair trade.

Finally, my boss kicked me out of the nest. I went straight to CNN and applied for a TV production job that I once would have dismissed as uncreative and mundane. I've had that job for a year and a half now, and I love it.

And my cranky ex-boss? I found out later that he gave me a stellar recommendation that helped me land the CNN gig. I owe him a lot.

Luis Rodriguez
Atlanta, GA

PART III

The New-Job Playbook

Fifty Winning Tactics You Probably Didn't Learn in School

Colleges (and even high schools) have been under fire lately for not teaching work-related skills. But what are "work-related skills"? In fact, most job skills are highly task-specific—cooking an omelet, calculating payroll deductions, designing an electronic circuit, writing computer code—and few of us will ever hold jobs where even the most basic competence in these skills has any relevance.

If you talk to employers, however, the skills gaps that often frustrate them have more to do with *general* areas of business-related competence—communication, organization, teamwork, basic finance, efficiency, problem-solving, and the like. Especially when jobs involve tasks with many moving parts and complex human interactions, schools are notoriously poor at delivering graduates with real-world skills in these areas.

For instance, Ken Kuang, the founder and president of a San Diego industrial materials firm, says he's constantly amazed by the lack of basic financial how-to knowledge he finds among graduates of major MBA programs:

You'd think that a profit-and-loss forecast would be a bedrock concept for a program teaching people to start their own businesses. You'd be wrong. I've mentored graduate students at prestigious universities who couldn't tell me how they were going to cover things like payroll taxes, workers' compensation and other costs. One had generously given himself a salary of $125,000 in his business plan and was astonished when I sat him down and showed him he'd be lucky to make $50,000 annually. Another didn't understand how retail pricing worked and couldn't believe how little his company would clear from a retailer like Walmart.

To fill these kinds of education gaps, it's usually up to the employer to provide on-the-job training—and to take the risk that the employee and the investment will walk out the door a year later.

No surprise: Any employee who shows up with basic competence in these general skills will stand out. If you're good at public speaking, organizing a complicated project, or interviewing a customer... then you'll probably get better assignments than your co-workers. If you know something about finance and statistics, you'll have an edge over all your co-workers who think "math is too hard." And over the whole arc of your career, this small edge will almost certainly put you way ahead of employees who never quite mastered ordinary business skills.

Of course, it's far beyond the scope of this book to give you a ground-up mastery of all the work-related skills you might need in a new job. Instead, we've tried to identify a set of 50 practical "playbook" tactics that should yield immediate results during your first hundred days. Pick out the skills you think you'll need the most and practice until you feel both proficient and confident. You'll be on your way.

—Jeffrey Tarter

How to Leverage an Internship

In several trades and professions (law, architecture, journalism, and many unionized building trades), interns get well-supervised, real-world experience and skills development. If you take part in this kind of program, you'll almost certainly be in good hands. However, many other organizations treat their interns as cheap (or even free) labor; you may spend your summer doing little more than making photocopies and going on lunch runs. Bad internships do have one great benefit: The victims will never again doubt the truth of a Dilbert cartoon.

Remember that your goal is to get *maximum value* out of your internship experience, so pay attention to these five tactics:

 First, interview the program manager: Interns tend to be too passive about their expectations. As soon as possible (before you even start work, if you can), have a conversation with whoever will be your immediate supervisor. Ask two questions: "What will I learn here?" and "What should I do to stand out?" If your supervisor can't give you a straight answer to both of these questions, politely escalate the question to a better-informed manager. If everyone seems clueless, that's a warning sign that the people you will work with don't have their internship act together. You still might get some value out of the time you invest, but you'll have to make it happen on your own.

Network like crazy: Make a point of having lunch with every manager you work with, and get them to tell you about their jobs, the industry, and how to be a star. By the end of your internship, you should have built a network of friends in your chosen industry who will tell you about future job openings and who may recommend you to their own circle of friends. As career advisors are fond of saying, "The one with the most connections wins."

(Incidentally, don't spend too much time socializing with your fellow interns. There's not much you can learn from them, and they'll be your competition when all of you are out looking for real jobs.)

✓ **Accomplish something memorable:** Remember that your internship should yield a very strong recommendation by the time you leave. So focus your efforts on developing a simple, clear story: "Sarabeth did an amazing job creating our new company Facebook page" is much more compelling than "Sarabeth was a very pleasant and helpful person to have around the office."

✓ **Be a perfectionist:** Yes, you'll be doing donkey work a lot of the time. But take that work seriously. If you make mistakes when you type up the schedule for the office baseball team, you won't get a shot at anything more interesting. And you'll annoy all the baseball players in your office as well.

Being a perfectionist also means showing up on time, keeping your desk organized, meeting deadlines, and otherwise acting like a professional. Says Matt Meuleners, a partner at Focus Training:

> Nothing demonstrates a lack of experience more than interns who think they can skip work like they skip class, roll in late because they were out until 2:00am, or rock the Girl Talk t-shirt in an office of crisp Brooks Brothers. Whether you collect a paycheck or not, an internship is a job and you can easily lose it. Or worse, you could spend an entire semester of your life at a company and *not* get a good reference.

✓ **Volunteer, volunteer, volunteer:** Every office has a backlog of mundane tasks that the regular employees never find time to complete. When you spot something that isn't getting done, raise your hand and offer to help. Assemble sales kits, install new software, update mailing lists, clean up after a big meeting, proofread product documentation, transcribe interview notes... promptly volunteer to do whatever needs to be done. As an intern, you might be given these chores anyway—but you'll earn bonus points for volunteering *before* you're asked.

How to Deliver a Compelling Presentation

Standing up in front of an audience may terrify you, but sooner or later you'll be asked to make presentations to co-workers, clients, and perhaps even senior management. You also may be asked to do demos and webinars, run training classes, moderate panels, and introduce speakers. If you try to beg off, you'll get the usual advice to nervous presenters: "Just imagine that everyone in the audience is stark naked." This is supposed to help?

In reality, public speaking is a *learned* skill. The more often you get in front of audiences, the more you'll feel comfortable and in control. You'll figure out what works, what engages your audience, which little tricks can improve your performance.

Public speaking is also an *important* skill. Most great leaders, influencers, teachers, celebrities, innovators, and successful artists and writers have learned to stand in front of an audience and deliver a powerful, persuasive, engaging talk. If you never master basic presentation skills, your career path is probably going to be limited.

Five useful tactics:

 Talk about what your listeners want to hear: Most of your audience will be too polite to complain that you're wasting their time. But they will stop listening to you if your talk isn't directly relevant to their personal interests. Lengthy textbook explanations, sales pitches, and evangelism are almost always a turnoff. Kelly Stoetzel, who preps speakers for the prestigious TED lecture series, cautions speakers against trying to hammer home a message. "Don't think, 'This is a message I must communicate,'" she says. "Instead, think 'People will love knowing about this!'"

If possible, try out your presentation theme (not the presentation itself) on three or four likely audience members. If they're not enthusiastic, ask what you're missing. Focus on content issues, not on delivery technology: Bad content can kill your talk, while ugly fonts will only annoy a few people.

Whenever you're speaking to a small group (say, 30 or fewer people) a good way to get your content on track is to invite questions right at the beginning, rather than holding a Q&A session after you've finished speaking. You'll find that early questions often trigger lively follow-on discussions among audience members, which you can moderate for a few minutes before returning to your main discussion thread. And be ready to edit the rest of your talk on the fly, based on issues that surface during early audience interaction. (This tactic is especially important when your presentation involves a scripted product demo or capabilities presentation. As quickly as possible, find out what your *prospect* wants to know and deliver a blow-their-socks-off answer to that specific question.)

✓ **Keep your story line simple:** Make sure the flow and logic of your talk are absolutely clear. A good reality test is to ask whether the title of your talk makes a promise that accurately describes the content of your talk: "Three Reasons Why Our Q4 Sales Are Up," "How We Improved Customer Satisfaction," "A Tour of Our New Retail Signage." If you can't sum up your subject in a few words, you should probably prune away a lot of the verbiage.

When you're explaining a fairly complex subject, often the best approach is literally to tell a story. The classic narrative formula is based on three parts:

- ➤ **Problem:** For example, "Our major maintenance clients were unhappy with support reps who didn't understand the client's business."
- ➤ **Search for a Solution:** "Our company researched dozens of possible solutions and decided to introduce business-savvy account managers."
- ➤ **Resolution:** "Our clients were delighted and renewals increased by 15%."

This formula underlies virtually every popular tale from Cinderella to the latest Law & Order episode... because it works.

And don't be afraid to build interest by incorporating characters, anecdotes, conflict, and other story-telling elements. BusinessWeek.com columnist Carmine Gallo points out that Steve Jobs—one of the technology world's most admired presenters—developed a narrative-based style that always left audiences spellbound:

> A Steve Jobs presentation has all the elements of a great movie—heroes and villains, stunning visuals, and a supporting cast. And, like a movie director, Steve Jobs 'storyboards' the plot... In every classic story, the hero fights the villain. The same holds true of a Steve Jobs presentation. In 1984, the villain was IBM, known as 'Big Blue' at the time. 'IBM wants it all,' he said. Apple would be the only company to stand in its way. It was very dramatic and the crowd went crazy.

✓ **Clean up your charts and graphs:** Numbers are tough to present in an interesting fashion. But a lot of corporate presentations exist largely to report trends, operating results, financial performance, and other numbers-intensive data. If you simply paste raw Excel output into PowerPoint, you'll be left with slides that your audience has to squint to see and information that you can't easily explain. "Here in cell C136 you'll notice that the error rate for last month is trending upward, compared to C126 and C116..." Is anyone listening?

Better: Learn how to create professional-looking charts and graphs from within Excel itself, which has reasonably good tools for managing color, fonts, 3D views, captions, and other effects. Add arrows and other highlights to demonstrate trends or items you want to explain. And take a close look at how popular business magazines and newspapers create "infographics" that tell a clear story about complex numbers. If your job calls for frequent number-crunching presentations, the time you spend learning to produce stronger charts and graphs is likely to be a wise investment.

✓ **Watch the clock:** Running out of time is a common failing of disorganized speakers, and a too-long talk usually disrupts everyone else's schedule. Motivational speaker Hugh Culver also points out that lack of time discipline can sabotage your main message:

> I don't know how many speakers I have seen rush through their last 15 slides, and in a panicked voice try to motivate an audience in three minutes... No one will miss what isn't there. Punch the number of your closing slide into the keyboard, jump to your close, and forget the rest.

If you're expected to do frequent short presentations — for instance, status reports, demos, new employee introductions — look into a popular new presentation format called PechaKucha. The discipline is simple: speakers get no more than 20 slides, with just 20 seconds to spend on each. Any concept or graphic that doesn't fit this format has to be cut or revised. Autodesk CEO Carl Bass is a big fan of PechaKucha, which he says "makes people crisp." He adds, "I won't tell you that PechaKucha prevents people from giving bad presentations. The good news is that they can give them for only six minutes and 40 seconds."

✓ **Maintain eye contact:** Good speakers never turn their back on the audience to read slides or look down at their notes. Never. Unbroken eye contact creates a sense of a one-on-one conversation between you and each listener, and very few audience members will turn away or otherwise disconnect if you're looking right at them.

How to Run a Great Meeting

Meetings are one of the most disliked parts of corporate life. However, meetings are also an essential way for team members to share information and ideas. Yes, you can conduct virtual meetings online, by email, or through various fancy collaboration tools. But if an issue really matters, you're going to want face-to-face discussion.

Trouble is, running a meeting is a skill that few managers have mastered. Too many monologs, too many attendees, too many low-value agenda items... and too little post-meeting action. If it weren't for the free donuts, the peasants would have revolted long ago.

As a newbie, you may be given a few of these miserable meetings to run. Here's how you can do the job better:

✓ **Think of your role as the meeting facilitator:** Traditionally, meetings are run by the team's boss or a senior manager. Bad idea: If you want an open discussion, putting the boss in charge discourages contrary opinions and encourages the showoffs. Instead, you should assume the role of a meeting "facilitator," whose primary goals are to get everyone talking and to reach consensus decisions. As you become more skilled as a facilitator, your boss will usually be delighted to turn the gavel over to you.

✓ **Control the agenda:** The only items that really belong on the agenda are topics that require broad discussion and decisions about actions. Routine status reports and announcements should be distributed through email or memos, unless a would-be presenter can legitimately justify a need for time on the agenda. (Of course, some people will pull rank on you, but that's okay. They'll get the point eventually.)

✓ **Build momentum for major decisions:** Once you cut back on the trivia, you'll have time for the team to discuss a few select topics — ideally, issues where there's already an emerging debate. (Patrick Lencioni, author of *Death by Meeting*, says the goal should be to replace "decorum with passion and conflict.") Announce these big topics in advance and invite participants to distribute position papers and fact sheets that will lay the groundwork for informed discussion. The people who care about the outcome will have to show up at the meeting or risk losing their case.

✓ **Appoint sub-committees:** Whenever a discussion gets bogged down, your best tool is likely to be a sub-committee of two or three team members who care strongly about the issue at hand. Invite them to discuss the problem offline and come back with a recommendation. If no one volunteers, simply report in the meeting summary that no consensus was achieved and invite your boss to make the decision.

✓ **Distribute an after-action report:** As soon as the meeting is over, send everyone (even non-attendees) a summary of decisions and action items. The action items should always designate what Apple Computer calls a "Directly Responsible Individual" (DRI), with a deadline if that's relevant. As the facilitator, you should check with each DRI for a status update, and make sure unfinished items appear on the agenda for the following meeting.

How to Become a Better Negotiator

Here's how columnist Chris Buckholz describes the widespread aversion to negotiation: "Whether it's a fear of confrontation, or simply the knowledge that they're weaklings who don't deserve to win, many people actively avoid situations that require negotiation, or plow through as quickly as possible, accepting the worst possible deals in exchange for getting it over with."

Sound about right?

Alas, if you have this kind of phobia about negotiating, you're at a severe disadvantage in the corporate world. Your own salary, sales to customers, purchases from vendors, the work you share with team members, decisions about quality, pricing, strategy... all involve important give and take with other people. You don't have to adopt the personality of a junkyard dog to succeed at negotiation—but you should learn a few basic guidelines:

✓ **Be prepared:** The best negotiators may seem to win by sheer force of personality—but the reality is that they've probably done obsessive amounts of homework before they sit down at the table. They know prevailing prices, they know their own company's costs and priorities, and they know who has actual decision-making authority on both sides. As a result of their deeper knowledge of possible deal parameters, top negotiators tend to control the discussion agenda right from the beginning.

✓ **Be ready with non-cash bargaining chips:** Rookie negotiators often fall into the trap of believing that all negotiations are simple win-lose battles over price. Master deal-makers know better: Buyers are often willing to pay a premium to get such benefits as a performance guarantee, extended payment terms, or free installation; sellers are likely to offer hefty discounts in return for being able to book a sale during the current quarter, for getting a strong customer testimonial, or for collecting cash up front. Bargaining chips like these will usually cost you almost nothing, but they may shake loose substantial price concessions from the other side.

In fact, using bargaining chips should become almost a habit. Ask for something in return — anything, really — whenever you're forced to lower a price or make a concession. Your boss says there's no money in the budget for the raise you deserve? Ask for a more impressive title or a glamorous assignment. A vendor won't budge on the price of license fees? Ask for extra seats, free training, or a discount on the next upgrade. Even tough negotiators don't want to poison an ongoing relationship, so they'll usually try to find a few tradeoffs that give you extra value for almost zero cost to themselves.

✓ **Avoid complex customization:** If you're negotiating a complex contract — say, for a multi-year software maintenance plan or a large-scale consulting project — there can be literally hundreds of tricky details. Rather than negotiate each element individually, start by presenting a well-documented "package" contract that spells out your company's preferred approach to all the key details. You'll still get pushback on a few negotiable points, but the customer will usually accept your approach for the vast majority of items.

✓ **Think past the handshake:** Serial entrepreneur and author James Altucher warns that a deal isn't final until all the documents are signed and the goods or services are delivered. This wrapup phase can be "excruciatingly painful," he says:

> Every day after agreement, make it a point to stay in touch, be friends, keep focusing on the vision (particularly with the champion for your deal on the other side), have just as much energy to close all the details, keep in touch with the lawyers to make sure paperwork is going through, keep working on the alternatives (since the negotiation is not done until it's DONE), and so on.

Be ready to say No: Your strongest bargaining position is always your ability to walk away from a lousy deal. Once you admit to your opposite negotiator that you "must" close a deal (or even mention that you have to catch a reserved flight home) you've lost all bargaining power.

How to Interview a Customer

In virtually every kind of business, there's a constant buzz of conversation between customers and employees. Those customers have many names—clients, shoppers, students, patients, subscribers, audience members, donors, visitors, voters, and so forth. But whatever you call your customers, the conversation usually starts this way:

CUSTOMER: "I need..."
EMPLOYEE: "Here's how we can help..."

If your job involves sales or customer service, you're likely to become pretty skillful at responding to common customer needs. You'll have standard scripts and training in the fine points of your company's products and solutions.

But if you're not part of your company's regular sales and services channels, you're still likely to have occasional customer conversations... and these conversations can alert you to problems your company ought to fix or inspire out-of-the-box ideas for new products or services.

However, marketing guru Kristin Zhivago, a veteran at interviewing customers, points out that getting great feedback takes a certain degree of interviewing skill:

> Your customers are the only ones who will tell you, willingly, what they want from you, and how they want to buy it, but only *if you ask them properly, in the right way, at the right time.*

Five tips on how to interview customers:

✓ **Create an interview checklist:** A good customer interview will feel like a spontaneous conversation, says Zhivago, but in fact you should start with a carefully structured list of "about ten to fifteen primary questions in a one-hour interview." One key question: *"What problem were you trying to solve?"* The goal here is to discover the specific way that customers think about their problems, and the actual terminology they use—

187

especially when using search engine key words to find solutions.

✓ **Explore relationship issues:** Customers are often influenced by much more than the specific value of a product or service. As part of your interview script, include a few questions about possible glitches in the buying process (was it hard to do business with us? did we answer your questions?) and customer service (did we treat you well after the sale?). Ask if there are important services that your customers would *like* you to provide. These requests may inspire new profit centers and also strengthen customer loyalty.

✓ **Identify major points of irritation:** *"If you were the CEO of our company, what's the first thing you'd focus on?"* That question "reveals what is most important in the customer's mind," says Zhivago. "I have found that customers are very consistent in their responses to this question. After even just a few interviews, you will see a definite theme."

✓ **Never get defensive:** The goal of an interview is to find out what the customer believes, and sometimes those beliefs are simply wrong or outdated, Zhivago points out. But never try to correct a customer's bone-headed mistake. "Interrupting will effectively end the interview," she warns. (You can go back and correct a faulty perception after the interview is over, however.)

✓ **Use the phone:** "People will say things on the phone they wouldn't dream of saying in an email or text message, an online survey, or a social media site," says Zhivago:

> This is especially true if you are selling a business-to-business product or service, but it applies to any type of consumer. People know that emails and instant messages are permanent and public forms of communication. They know that whatever they say in text form could well be 'on the record.' So they hold back.

How to Manage a Project

"Project" is a word that's come to mean any fairly complex task with a well-defined deadline and some degree of customization. Building a house is a project, running a conference is a project, defending a lawsuit is a project. Most projects involve teams of people working together, but it's also common to find one- and two-person projects that are assigned to fairly junior employees. Your primary goal is to complete the project successfully, of course. But your boss will also keep an eye on how you manage schedules, budgets, change requests, and other implementation details. Here's where you can build your project management skills and reputation quickly.

Five useful tactics:

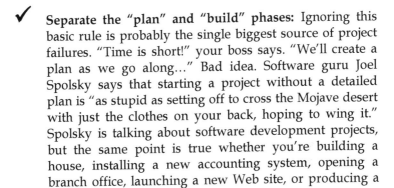

Separate the "plan" and "build" phases: Ignoring this basic rule is probably the single biggest source of project failures. "Time is short!" your boss says. "We'll create a plan as we go along..." Bad idea. Software guru Joel Spolsky says that starting a project without a detailed plan is "as stupid as setting off to cross the Mojave desert with just the clothes on your back, hoping to wing it." Spolsky is talking about software development projects, but the same point is true whether you're building a house, installing a new accounting system, opening a branch office, launching a new Web site, or producing a movie.

So do whatever it takes to make sure you start with a plan that's explicit about what you're expected to do, what the job will cost, and how long it will take. And get signoffs on these details from each and every stakeholder before any implementation work starts. (This assumes that you have meaningful authority as part of your role as project manager. In real life, project managers are often just paper pushers... which perhaps explains why their projects go off a cliff.)

✓ **Build a checklist:** Checklists are a deceptively simple tool for managing complex, highly-detailed projects and tasks. Atul Gawande, a practicing surgeon and best-selling author, points out that checklists have become a standard fail-safe routine for airplane pilots, building contractors, and (more recently) medical teams, rock concert producers, and venture capitalists. In *The Checklist Manifesto*, Gawande argues that checklists are particularly valuable for catching errors that occur when we're performing very routine, familiar tasks:

> Checklists seem to provide protection against such failures. They remind us of the minimum necessary steps and make them explicit. They not only offer the possibility of verification but also instill a kind of discipline of higher performance.

The most effective checklists, Gawande points out, usually reflect research into the likely failure points in a process and offer clear, brief instructions about how to fix the problem. Gawande adds that checklists are often a great way to get "multiple pairs of eyes on a problem" and to get team members to talk about working together, rather than focusing on their individual roles.

✓ **Remember that change orders are your friend:** Even if you have a detailed spec for the project, it's almost inevitable that your client (internal or external) will want to tweak the plan. It's fine to be accommodating — but always get the client to sign off on a formal change order. Moreover, the change order should itemize both the cost of the change *and* the impact on the project completion date. Making "little" changes without change orders can easily expand your costs to a point where the project actually loses money and misses its deadline. This is called "scope creep," and it's how the nice tool shed you were building turned into a five-car garage.

✓ **Resist using bodies to solve schedule slippage:** Back in 1974, a veteran IBM program manager wrote a slender book called *The Mythical Man-Month*. Frederick P. Brooks,

Jr., analyzed several major IBM software and hardware projects and summed up his findings with this now-classical aphorism: "The bearing of a child takes nine months, no matter how many women are assigned." In other words, Brooks said, any gains achieved by adding staff to a complex project tend to be lost in the greater overhead of managing more people. When schedules slip, he says,

> ...the natural (and traditional) response is to add manpower. Like dowsing a fire with gasoline, this makes matters worse, much worse. More fire requires more gasoline, and this begins a regenerative cycle which ends in disaster.

Now, it turns out that Brooks' principle allows for some exceptions. If you double the headcount on a 25-person project, you *might* see some modest gains on the schedule. But adding 25 more people to your project will blow your budget through the roof, and nobody is going to give 25 bodies to a rookie project manager anyway. If your schedule is slipping, look for different solutions (for instance, cutting back the scope to eliminate unnecessary frills).

✓ **Schedule a punch list phase:** In the construction industry, a "punch list" is a final itemized report of small tasks that haven't been completed (or completed properly) — missing hardware, uneven paint, a defective appliance. Adding a formal punch list phase to other kinds of projects is also a good practice, especially when you're trying to keep track of multiple team workers and a maze of little details — software bugs, typos in documents, illegible charts, and the like. Do a thorough walkthrough of the final deliverable as it will look from the client's or user's perspective, and then make sure all the glitches are fixed.

If you've been checking your work on a daily or weekly schedule, you may not find many punch list items to correct. But even with excellent quality assurance, you should always allow plenty of time for the punch list phase. Experienced project managers joke about how "the

last 1% of a project takes 50% of the time to complete"...
but there's a nugget of truth in their humor. Plan
accordingly.

How to Manage a Budget

As a newbie, you'll probably have a bare minimum of budget authority. You might keep track of a small project budget, a few team members, or a personal expense account. Petty cash, in other words.

But managing budgets (or pieces of budgets) is a big deal in virtually every business. Making sensible choices about money is a core skill if you expect to get promoted; handling money carelessly will mark you as a risky bet.

Five tips:

✓ **Make sure your major expenditures are driving sales and profits:** Think of your budget as a mini-business (otherwise called a "profit center"). Your goal is to spend money to produce results — sales, leads, client deliverables, enhanced reputation, etc. Depending on company policy, you may have a green light to spend *some* of your budget on intangibles like "good will" and "team morale" — but check first. Otherwise you may not be reimbursed for that $200 bottle of wine you bought to celebrate your team's first $100,000 sale.

✓ **Don't use the budget to micro-manage:** "I see budgets all the time that show line items for every magazine subscription and pizza party," says financial consultant Michael Gonnerman. "This is just silly. Budget managers should focus on how much money they need within broad categories, and should have discretionary power to move money around within these categories during the year." (Your boss or your CFO can probably give you a standard template that lays out the company's preferred format.)

✓ **Track labor hours closely:** Many companies — for instance, building contractors, consultants, creative services firms, programming shops — prefer to base their budgets on the estimated hours that each task requires.

There are often very detailed benchmarks for the amount of time specific tasks should take, so it's easy to take those benchmarks and multiply them by the company's actual hourly pay, profit margin, and overhead numbers.

Even if you don't use labor hours directly in your budgets, it's often better to measure efficiency gains on a budgeted task in average hours rather than dollars. "We cut two hours off each installation job" is much easier to understand than "We've reduced costs on the installation line item by $1,527 to $2,202, depending on which technician is doing the work."

Be particularly careful when you calculate the amount of time you budget for overhead hours. Overhead includes birthday parties, fire drills, staff meetings, training classes, vacations, travel, and other time when your team members aren't actually cranking out billable work. A standard rule of thumb is that overhead hours usually represent about 40% of a team's available work time. Clients and bosses will insist that the number should be lower, and sometimes they're right. But not often.

✓ **Hang on to the check book:** Here's a scenario you never want to happen: You come back from running a successful conference, and you discover thousands of dollars in extra charges on the hotel invoice: audio-visual equipment, bar bills, limo services, room service banquets... all signed for by members of your staff. Since you neglected to tell the hotel that only you should be allowed to sign for expenses outside the conference contract, you (and your budget) are stuck with the extra costs. And when your boss finds out... well, it won't be a happy conversation.

The simple rule: Never delegate the right to approve expenses to *anyone*.

✓ **Rank your expenses by annual dollar amount:** Your regular financial reports will show you where you're spending money by category. That's handy, but you should also see where your biggest individual expenses occur — for instance, items like travel, printing, advertising, or overnight shipping. Get your team together and brainstorm some cheaper, out-of-the-box alternatives. If you can save 10% on even a few of your biggest expenses, that's going to drop an impressive amount of profit to your budget's bottom line.

How to Interpret Survey Data

More than ever, companies now make major decisions based on survey data — customer satisfaction polls, industry benchmarking studies, salary surveys, feedback from sales reps, employee morale trend analysis, and the like. One reason for the influential role of surveys is that surveys *feel* authoritative. The data comes from people who are presumably real customers or independent experts, the numbers look like precise mathematical calculations (often carried out to several decimal places), and the company probably spent a bundle of cash to get the results. Who would dare question the validity of the data?

In fact, an old rule of thumb often applies: "Garbage in, garbage out." If your new job involves working with survey data, be skeptical about the quality of the data you'll be using when you make decisions.

Here are five recommendations for interpreting survey data:

✓ **First, ask tough questions about methodology:** Survey results can vary greatly depending on how and when the data is collected. If the survey report doesn't clearly tell you about methodology — and many don't — make sure the whole process passes the sniff test. Does the survey manager have a vested interest? Are the respondents likely to give honest answers? Is the data presented professionally (e.g., are medians and error ranges used correctly)?

"It's a common belief that different survey methodologies will cause only trivial differences in results," says survey designer and analyst Frederick Van Bennekom. "In reality, small differences in methodology can produce enormous variations — sometimes so great that you can't even guess at the 'true' numbers."

✓ **Check out the sample makeup:** Survey data can be useful even if relatively few people are polled — *if* those people have the same characteristics as the larger universe you're trying to analyze. For instance, Phil Verghis points out that tech support satisfaction scores are typically based on a "tiny fraction of customers who ever contact you, even when they have a problem. Of this tiny fraction, an even tinier fraction are people who will respond to your survey on how 'happy' they are. Are these survey respondents representative of a company's whole customer base? Probably not," says Verghis.

✓ **Read the survey questionnaire:** Be sure to check the wording of the original survey questions against the brief report labels that usually describe survey results. You may find a significant mismatch between the questionnaire language (which is what the respondent actually saw) and the summary. Worse, you may find that the questionnaire's language is so vague and confusing that the answers are likely to be worthless.

✓ **Pay attention to free text comments:** A good survey will often suggest a list of possible answers, which helps put the respondent's answers into easily-measured buckets. That's okay — but sometimes the survey author leaves out important possibilities. That's when it's valuable to include "free-text" comments as a response option. Be sure to read through these comments (and similar discussions on company forums) for fresh perspectives on the survey-based decisions you're trying to make.

✓ **Watch for bumpy trendlines:** A one-time survey is often untrustworthy or hard to interpret. The best surveys are conducted over and over, with minimal tweaking of the survey questions or sample characteristics. This repetition will let you spot important trends that need action, and will give you a reliable measure of the effectiveness of changes you make in company operations. Of course, if all the responses bounce around from survey to survey, that's usually a sign that your raw data is mostly just noise. Ditch the survey and start over.

How to Build a Business Forecast

Successful companies constantly hunt for "better mousetraps." From the CEO to the greenest rookie (that's you), their employees are encouraged to invent better systems, better product features, better marketing tactics. Even if most of these ideas are duds, a few spectacular winners are bound to surface.

But corporate innovation isn't the same as haphazard brainstorming. Rick Kilton, a veteran leadership coach, points out that "unstructured" employee ideas rarely survive close scrutiny:

> [Employees] often create ideas from the negative emotions that occur when something interferes with their work or quality of life. Employees also tend to take a myopic view, and their ideas do not consider the organization as a whole.

Kilton points out that the ideas that are taken most seriously by upper management tend to involve corporate priorities — in particular, growing revenues, cutting costs, and boosting productivity. And ideas almost always have to pass a "return on investment" (ROI) test, which is essentially a forecast of likely implementation costs vs. potential profits. Companies develop ROI forecasts in different ways, but once you learn to create a basic forecast model your suggestions will begin to attract more serious attention.

Five tips:

 Make investment decisions based on profits, not payback: Imagine you've just been hired as an assistant manager at The Breakfast Barn. A restaurant equipment sales rep drops by to show you an automated pancake machine that costs $10,000. "This machine will pay for itself in just ten months," the sales rep promises. "That's less than $35 in incremental pancake sales per day!" Is this a deal you should bring to your boss?

Well, no. Your boss will probably point out that most of the sales rep's "$35 per day" in new revenue will have to cover the cost of *making* the additional pancakes. "We'd only clear about $5 a day in profits on the extra revenue. If you run the numbers, you'll see that it will take more than five *years* just to break even on the nifty machine you're recommending. I think we'll keep making pancakes on the grill the old-fashioned way."

✓ **Show your work:** Burke Franklin, whose company develops widely-used business planning software, points out that financial forecasts are only as good as the underlying data and assumptions:

> Every good financial plan begins by introducing and explaining the major business assumptions you used to make your projections. Your business assumptions are what you must sell investors; the rest is arithmetic. Every assumption needs to withstand the challenge, 'How did you figure that?'

The problem, of course, is that you often can't find data that will support your assumptions. We tend to believe that *somewhere* the exact data we need can be found (everything is on Google, isn't it?). But good data costs money to compile, and sometimes it just doesn't exist in any form that directly supports your forecast. To make your case, you may have to get creative about using sketchy data that only supports your assumptions indirectly.

✓ **Test the waters:** Usually, the best way to generate persuasive forecast data is to run a small-scale pilot program. Try out a vendor's new productivity gizmo in a few low-profile offices, test a price increase only in your North Dakota stores, run a randomized A/B test of your new vs. old Web landing pages for a week or two. You'll generate real numbers that are far more meaningful than saying, "We talked to five industry analysts and they all validated our concept" (whatever that means).

✓ **Try to quantify the risk factors:** If you're creating a forecast that involves significant cash outlays and effort, it's best to present at least three scenarios (optimistic, pessimistic, and most likely) and ideally a few more that reflect uncertainties in each of your most important variables. If you've done your homework on risk factors, you'll be prepared to answer a surprisingly broad range of what-if questions. What's the ROI if the price of ingredients in your proposed SpamBurger goes up? What if our competition starts a price war with us? What if it takes twice as long to migrate users to our new service?

Remember that big-company managers are highly sensitive to risks, both to their careers and to the company's bottom line. You may forecast a fantastic ROI for your proposal, but the decision-makers are likely to kill any suggestion that exposes the company to an open-ended, poorly defined risk.

✓ Avoid "stretch" goals: A forecast is not supposed to be wishful thinking. Presenting rosy numbers may help you sell your idea in the beginning, but you're setting yourself up for failure if the actual outcome falls short of your forecast. People who consistently hit their forecast numbers are trusted with bigger projects; those who over-promise rarely get a second chance.

How to Manage Your Time

Time management is probably the world's most-studied workplace skill. A typical bookstore will carry dozens of books on how to avoid procrastination, get more done in less time, control your calendar, reduce stress, and otherwise take charge of your daily life. If that's not enough advice for you, Amazon lists 5,226 "time management" titles and another 2,759 on "personal time management."

With all this attention, you'd think the corporate world would be well on the way to solving the time management challenge. But you'd be wrong. Franklin Covey, a $200 million vendor of day-planners, training, and consulting, recently found that the 350,000 respondents to a global time management survey still feel that they spend an average of 40% of their time on tasks that are "unimportant or irrelevant" to their work. Where are the rocket scientists when we need them?

As a very junior employee, you'll quickly spot one of the biggest obstacles to basic time management: the people you work with. Regardless of how disciplined you are, your day is likely to be interrupted constantly by emails, meetings, phone calls, client requests, status questions, and minor emergencies. None of these interruptions are important to *you*, which is why you'd count them as part of the Franklin Covey 40% of time that's "unimportant or irrelevant."

Trouble is, these interruptions are important to the people you work with—and most of these people outrank you. So you're not going to find a magic formula for making interruptions go away. The best you can accomplish, probably, is to organize the time you actually control a little better.

Some tips:

 Keep a diary: Make a brief note of everything you do during your working day. Then add a star next to any item you think qualifies as a significant accomplishment. Not enough stars? Invest some time in figuring out what's keeping you from earning more personal stars: That's probably the root cause you need to address. And if you don't have the power to solve this problem, talk to your boss about the tradeoffs you're being forced to make between time-wasting tasks and the results you're supposed to deliver.

✓ **Save high-energy times for important tasks:** If you're a morning person, come in early, close your door, and spend a couple of hours creating a great client presentation or designing a brilliant new product interface. After your brain is fried, then deal with your email, return calls, and hold minor meetings. Or if you get revved up in the afternoon, reverse this order. Naturally, you'll still have some conflicts with other people who insist on interrupting you. Your polite answer: "I'm in the middle of something here I need to finish. Can we talk after lunch?" Unless the building is on fire, most of your co-workers will honor your request.

✓ **Respond quickly, solve slowly:** "Crisis" interruptions are likely to be the most difficult to handle. A customer is outraged by an unexpected invoice, a seminar speaker has cancelled, a critical delivery is late... and it's up to you to drop everything and solve the problem. But here's what's usually happening: The person with the problem wants you to *acknowledge* their problem, not necessarily to *solve* it instantly. Find out what the real urgency is, and then schedule a time to discuss solutions. "Give me a little time to find out what's going on at our end and then let's talk at 3:00pm — okay?" Presto! You've just transformed an emergency into a scheduled part of the day's workflow. And you'll probably deliver a better solution than you would if you were scrambling to solve a crisis.

(Yes, you should respond immediately to any truly urgent crisis. But if your department is dealing with more than one hair-on-fire emergency a week, that's likely to be a management problem. Talk to your boss about what's going on.)

✓ **Track your email reply time:** You probably can't do much to cut back the time you spend reading your incoming email. But the real email black hole is more likely to be the time you spend *replying* to low-priority mail. Do you really need a long, thoughtful reply to every multi-recipient message that hits your inbox? Do you need to fill out every "brief" survey? Should you offer edits to every draft report and proposal that other teams circulate (respond to your own team's drafts, of course)? To check how much time you're spending on email replies, create a simple log and write down the number of minutes you spend on each reply for a week or two. Then get tough about spending more than a few minutes answering low-value messages. You may save upwards of an hour a day with this kind of self-discipline.

✓ **Make one networking contact every day:** When you're feeling squeezed for time, it's natural to cut back on "personal" stuff. Pretty soon you feel guilty about how you've lost touch with old friends and business connections. Of course, feeling guilty solves nothing... but it may help to set a purely arbitrary quota of one "touching base" contact (anything from a quick email to a lunch invitation) every day. That's roughly 300 contacts per year, which ought to be enough to keep your networking relationships in good health.

Notes & Sources

CHAPTER 1: The First Hundred Days

Napoleon swept back into power... Claire Suddath, "The 100-Day Benchmark," *Time*, April 29, 2009 (content.time.com/time/nation/article/0,8599,1894531,00.html). "The 100-day timeline can be traced back to Napoleon Bonaparte, because that's how long it took him to return from exile, reinstate himself as ruler of France and wage war against the English and Prussian armies before his final defeat at the Battle of Waterloo. (It actually took 111 days, but we'll give him a mulligan.)"

Franklin Roosevelt rolled out... Claire Suddath, "The 100-Day Benchmark," *Time*, April 29, 2009 (content.time.com/time/nation/article/0,8599,1894531,00.html). "By the time he hit the 100-day mark, Roosevelt had instituted the 'fireside chat' tradition, called Congress into a three-month-long special session and passed 15 pieces of major legislation—the beginning of what would come to be known as the New Deal—which created everything from the Tennessee Valley Authority to the Federal Deposit Insurance Corporation. With farm credits, federal works projects and new financial regulations in place, the U.S. of June 1933 was a substantially different place from that of 100 days earlier."

It's not a perfect measure... Kenneth T. Walsh, "The First 100 Days," *U.S. News*, February 12, 2009. (www.usnews.com/news/history/articles/2009/02/12/the-first-100-days-franklin-roosevelt-pioneered-the-100-day-concept).

New companies terminate roughly a quarter... Stephanie Gleason and Rachel Feintzeig, "At Startups, Pink Slips Come Early and Often," *The Wall Street Journal*, December 13, 2013. (www.wsj.com/news/articles/SB20001424052702304202204579254540454121188)

CHAPTER 2: Your Boss

Management guru Peter Drucker... Peter Drucker, "Managing Oneself," originally published in *The Harvard Business Review*, January 1999; reprinted in *On Managing Yourself,* Harvard Business Review Press (2010).

Leadership IQ found that 26% of failures... "Why New Hires Fail," Leadership IQ, (www.leadershipiq.com/blogs/leadershipiq/35354241-why-new-hires-fail-emotional-intelligence-vs-skills).

According to an Inc. Magazine survey... Maeghan Ouimet, "Jerk Alert: The Real Cost of Bad Bosses," *Inc. Magazine*, November 2012 (www.inc.com/maeghan-ouimet/real-cost-bad-bosses.html)

One management consulting firm even found... Lynn Taylor Consulting (www.lynntaylorconsulting.com).

Executive coach Bruce Tulgan claims... Bruce Tulgan, *It's Okay to Manage Your Boss*, 2010.

Admiral Grace Hopper once said... quoted in *Built to Learn*, by Cliff Purington, Chris Butler, and Sarah Fister Gale (2003).

Career guru Donald Asher points out... Donald Asher, *Who Gets Promoted* (2007).

CHAPTER 3: Your Team

Adam Smith's example of an 18th Century Scottish pin factory... Adam Smith, *An Inquiry into the Nature and Causes of the Wealth of Nations* (1776).

An ability to leverage the performance of a team... Yves Morieux, a senior partner at the Boston Consulting Group (Washington, DC), points out that a French relay race team managed to win a world championship against a U.S. team whose individual runners were much faster – because the French team was much quicker at handing off the baton. "How Too Many Rules at Work Keep You From Getting Things Done," TED, July 20, 2015 (https://www.ted.com/talks/yves_morieux_how_too_many_rules_at_work_keep_you_from_getting_things_done?language=en).

The Borg Collective... In the Star Trek universe, the Borg are "the forced combined consciousness of trillions of individuals, using technology. The Borg are distinguished by their collective consciousness (often heard by a chorus of voices), their fusion of biological matter and technology, and their driving principle to assimilate all knowledge or eradicate threats, without regard to ethics." Star Trek Wiki (sto.gamepedia.com/Borg_Collective).

Peter Drucker points out... Peter Drucker, "Managing Oneself," originally published in *The Harvard Business Review*, January 1999; reprinted in *On Managing Yourself*, Harvard Business Review Press (2010).

Carnegie Mellon professor Robert Kelley... Robert E. Kelley, *How to Be a Star at Work* (1999).

According to Phil Verghis... Phil Verghis, CEO, Klever, Chapel Hill, NC.

Says Michelle Lederman... Michelle Lederman, *The 11 Laws of Likability* (2012).

Research consistently shows that teams underperform... Diane Coutu, "Why Teams Don't Work," an interview with J. Richard Hackman, originally published in *The Harvard Business Review*, May 2009; reprinted in On Teams, Harvard Business Review Press (2013).

Jeff Bezos has a similar "two-pizza" rule... Rich Karlgaard, "Think (Really) Small," *Forbes*, April 13, 2015 (www.forbes.com/sites/richkarlgaard/2015/04/01/think-really-small/).

A mentoring relationship usually depends on personal chemistry... Ross McCammon, "Gray Matters," *Entrepreneur Magazine*, January 2014.

Here's how Dr. Marie McIntyre describes the payoff... Marie G. McIntyre, Ph.D., *Secrets to Winning at Office Politics* (2005).

"The Godfather Rule"... Inspired by a classic movie trilogy and best-selling novel about the Mafia, the Godfather story suggests interesting insights into corporate politics. For more on this topic, see Iris Milanova, "15 Life Lessons from the Godfather" (thoughtcatalog.com/iris-milanova/2014/01/15-life-lessons-from-the-godfather).

According to Dale Carnegie... Dale Carnegie, *How to Win Friends and Influence People* (1936; revised 1981). Hugely influential and still an essential guide to personal relationships.

People who complain about everything ... Chester Elton, "7 Things Motivated People Don't Do," LinkedIn Pulse, September 11, 2014 (https://www.linkedin.com/pulse/20140911163803-39785422-7-things-motivated-people-don-t-do).

Lee Iacocca recalls... Lee Iacocca, *Where Have All the Leaders Gone?* (2007).

At Morgan Stanley, a special mentoring track... Derek Loosvelt, "Q&A With Rani Nazim, a Female Executive Director at Morgan Stanley," Vault Blogs, October 23, 2013 (www.vault.com/blog/workplace-issues/qa-with-rani-nazim-a-female-executive-director-at-morgan-stanley).

Even asking for help with a tough decision... Ross McCammon, "Gray Matters," *Entrepreneur Magazine,* January 2014.

A conversation about pricing... "Price Fixing," Federal Trade Commission (https://www.ftc.gov/tips-advice/competition-guidance/guide-antitrust-laws/dealings-competitors/price-fixing).

Respect everyone, says office etiquette advisor Clinton Greenleaf... Clinton T. Greenleaf III, *The Unwritten Rules of the Workplace* (2010).

Create a special frequent contact circle... Tim Sanders, *The Likeability Factor* (2006).

Quit assuming that tools create connections... Jeff Haden, "The Only Networking Tips You Will Ever Need (to Build REAL Connections)," *LinkedIn Pulse*, March 4, 2015 (https://www.linkedin.com/pulse/only-networking-tips-you-ever-need-build-real-jeff-haden).

Become what he calls a "relentless giver"... Mark Babbitt, "Beyond Networking: 5 Ways Social Media Builds Your Brand," YouTern SavyIntern blog, June 8, 2015 (www.youtern.com/thesavvyintern/index.php/2015/06/08/beyond-networking-5-ways-social-media-builds-your-brand).

CHAPTER 5: Tasks vs. Results

Marketing guru Theodore Levitt made this point... Theodore Levitt, *The Marketing Imagination* (1983; revised 1986).

Scott McKelvey says he was thinking... Scott McKelvey, "Why That Whole 'People Don't Want a Drill, They Want a Hole' Thing Doesn't Go Far Enough," Web.Search.Social, August 8, 2012 (www.websearchsocial.com/why-that-whole-people-dont-want-a-drill-they-want-a-hole-thing-doesnt-go-far-enough).

TV cartoon show South Park... A long-running adult animated sitcom developed for the Comedy Central television network (southpark.cc.com). The Underpants Gnomes profit plan: https://www.youtube.com/watch?v=tO5sxLapAts.

As Woody Allen famously remarked... In his At the Helm blog, Bob Roitblat of the Mainsail Consulting Group points out that Woody Allen probably didn't originate the best-known version of his "showing up" quote, though he may have made similar remarks that were later combined into this version (www.atthehelmblog.com/2013/03/03/woody-allens-success-secrets).

That's especially true of manual work... George Anders, "McDonald's Jobs Taught Bezos, Leno and Others 7 Big Lessons," Forbes.com (www.forbes.com/sites/georgeanders/2012/07/24/mcdonalds-jobs). "Get really good at your routines; the world rewards order and discipline. Amazon's Jeff Bezos remembers learning, at age 16, how to crack eggs neatly with one hand. 'My favorite shift was Saturday morning,' he recalls. 'I would get a big bowl and crack 300 eggs in it.' That fastidiousness — and desire to operate on a huge scale — has marked Bezos's career ever since."

Raman K. Attri points out that one-size-fits-all corporate training classes... Personal correspondence, June 17, 2015.

Chester Elton says his research teams have found... Chester Elton, "7 Things Motivated People Don't Do," *LinkedIn Pulse*, September 11, 2014 (https://www.linkedin.com/pulse/20140911163803-39785422-7-things-motivated-people-don-t-do).

Another tantalizing research conclusion... Jeffrey Pfeffer and Sanford DeVoe, "When Is Happiness About How much You Earn? The effect of Hourly Payment on the Money-Happiness Connection," Personality and Social Psychology Bulletin, December 2009.

Elliot Weissbluth argues that it's a myth... Elliot Weissbluth, "If I Were 22: You Want to Change the World, Do You? Then Unlearn These 3 Things Now," Huffington Post, May 21, 2014 (www.huffingtonpost.com/elliot-s-weissbluth/if-i-were-22-you-want-to-millenials_b_5360986.html).

A good place to learn more... Kalid Azad, Better Explained (betterexplained.com).

Big law firms are particularly aggressive about time management... Janice Mucalov, LL.B, "Guide to Time Management for Lawyers," CBA PracticeLink (www.cba.org/cba/practicelink/cs/timemgmt.aspx).

Most important, says consultant and author Greg McKeown... Greg McKeown, "The Difference Between Successful And Very Successful People," Greg McKeown Blog, August 25, 2014 (gregmckeown.com/blog/difference-successful-successful-people).

According to Tony Schwartz and Catherine McCarthy... Tony Schwartz and Catherine McCarthy, "Managing Your Energy, Not Your Time," originally published in *The Harvard Business Review*, October 2007; reprinted in *On Managing Yourself*, Harvard Business Review Press (2010) (https://hbr.org/2007/10/manage-your-energy-not-your-time).

47% of current jobs are at high risk... Carl Benedikt Frey and Michael Osborne, *The Future Of Employment: How Susceptible Are Jobs To Computerisation?* (2013).

James Altucher warns that a widespread new paradigm... James Altucher, "10 Reasons Why You Have to Quit Your Job This Year," JamesAltucher.com, January 11, 2013 (www.jamesaltucher.com/2013/01/10-reasons-why-you-have-to-quit-your-job-this-year).

Patrick Lencioni says that one of the major reasons... Patrick Lencioni, *The Three Signs of a Miserable Job* (2007).

Jack Welch echoes this point... Jack Welch, "'Rank-and-Yank'? That's Not How It's Done," *The Wall Street Journal*, November 4, 2013 (www.wsj.com/articles/SB10001424052702303789604579198281053673534).

CHAPTER 6: Performance Metrics

Up or out career policy... Michael C. Jensen, "Tenure and Up-or-Out Promotion Systems," *Foundations of Organizational Strategy* (1998). From Wikipedia: "In a hierarchical organization, 'up or out', also known as a tenure or partnership system, is the requirement that each member of the organization must achieve a certain rank within a certain period of time. If they fail to do so, they must leave the organization... Accounting, consulting, law, and engineering are some industries in which this culture exists, tacitly or openly. Many military systems and academia also exhibit characteristics of the system." (https://en.wikipedia.org/wiki/Up_or_out).

Even better, says financial advisor Michael Gonnerman... Michael Gonnerman, *Ask Mike* (2012) (www.gonnerman.com/book.htm).

Too often, appraisal destroys human spirit... Tom Coens and Mary Jenkins, *Abolishing Performance Appraisals* (2000).

They get what they pay for... Alfie Kohn, *Punished by Rewards* (1993).

Inputs vs. outputs... Adam Bluestein, "Myth: Innovation is Costly," *Inc. Magazine*, September 2013 (www.inc.com/magazine/201309/less-innovation-is-better.html). "In its annual Global Innovation 1000 study, the consulting group Booz & Company has consistently found no correlation between a company's research and development spending and how innovative it is ranked by peers. What's more, it has found no relationship between R&D dollars and financial performance. In Booz's most recent survey, from 2012, the top 10 R&D spenders actually underperformed their industry peers in terms of both market capitalization and revenue growth."

A nifty collection of productivity tips... Jeremy Eden and Terri Long, *Low-Hanging Fruit* (2014).

CHAPTER 7: Figuring Out What Matters

An obscure Nordstrom's shoe salesman... Robert Spector and Patrick D. McCarthy, *The Nordstrom Way to Customer Service Excellence: The Handbook For Becoming the "Nordstrom" of Your Industry* (2012).

Companies typically pay bonuses... Bob Nelson, *1001 Ways to Reward Employees* (1994).

Howard Schultz, the visionary CEO... David A. Kaplan, "Starbucks: The Art of Endless Transformation," *Inc. Magazine*, June 2014 (www.inc.com/magazine/201406/david-kaplan/howard-schultz-reinvents-starbucks-constantly.html).

Even well-run companies suffer from problems... Cynthia Shapiro, *Corporate Confidential* (2005).

CHAPTER 8: First Impressions

Human beings often make snap judgments... Patti Wood, *SNAP* (2012); Michelle Trudeau, "You Had Me at Hello: The Science Behind First Impressions," NPR Shots, May 5, 2014 (www.npr.org/sections/health-shots/2014/05/05/308349318/you-had-me-at-hello-the-science-behind-first-impressions).

People who run large organizations... Charles Murray, *The Curmudgeon's Guide to Getting Ahead* (2014).

People use humor to build rapport... Fay Vincent, "Ten Tips for New Executives," *The Wall Street Journal*, February 3, 2014 (www.wsj.com/articles/SB10001424052702303519404579353060931625306).

That's the main source of the problem... Mark Bauerlein, "What Do U.S. College Graduates Lack? Professionalism," Bloomberg View, May 8, 2013 (www.bloombergview.com/articles/2013-05-08/what-do-u-s-college-graduates-lack-professionalism).

Work the house... Terry Stoetzel, "Secrets of a Great TED Talk," *Inc. Magazine*, October 2013.

Qualities in a professional services provider... Alexander Consulting, "Client Expectations of Consultants," (1995). Unpublished survey data.

Recommendations by a "likable" speaker... Sue Shellenbarger, "Why Likability Matters More Than Ever at Work," *The Wall Street Journal*, March 26, 2014 (www.wsj.com/articles/SB10001424052702303725404579461351615271292).

In case you need to brush up... Michelle Lederman, *The 11 Laws of Likability* (2012).

Routinely check your background online... William Arruda, Reach Personal Branding (www.reachpersonalbranding.com). Webinar presentation.

The social interactions when people ask for advice... Alison Wood Brooks and Francesca Gino, "Smart People Ask for (My) Advice: Seeking Advice Boosts Perceptions of Competence," *Management Science* 61, no. 6, June 2015.

CHAPTER 9: Building Your Brand

The world is full of outstanding performers... Donald Asher, *Who Gets Promoted* (2007).

Unique selling proposition... "The unique selling proposition (USP) or unique selling point is a marketing concept first proposed as a theory to explain a pattern in successful advertising campaigns of the early 1940s. The USP states that such campaigns made unique propositions to customers that convinced them to switch brands. The term was developed by television advertising pioneer Rosser Reeves of Ted Bates & Company. Theodore Levitt, a professor at Harvard Business School, suggested that, 'Differentiation is one of the most important strategic and tactical activities in which companies must constantly engage.' The term has been used to describe one's 'personal brand' in the marketplace." Wikipedia (https://en.wikipedia.org/wiki/Unique_selling_proposition).

The words have to emerge spontaneously... Dorie Clark, "Reinventing Your Personal Brand," *Harvard Business Review*, March 2011 (https://hbr.org/2011/03/reinventing-your-personal-brand/ar/1).

Make your message relevant... Andrea Coville, *Relevance* (2014).

The Food Network's Restaurant Impossible show... Dennis Wilson, "The Business Turnaround Tactics of Restaurant: Impossible's Robert Irvine," *Fast Company*, July 30, 2012 (www.fastcompany.com/1844041/business-turnaround-tactics-restaurant-impossibles-robert-irvine).

Working for a business unit that's in trouble... Donald Asher, *Who Gets Promoted* (2007).

Never tell anything that you'd like to keep secret... Cynthia Shapiro, *Corporate Confidential* (2005).

CHAPTER 10: Looking Like a Leader

The importance of the impression you make... Michael Watkins, *The First 90 Days* (2013).

You'll get more support from your boss... Cynthia Shapiro, *Corporate Confidential* (2005).

Dick Costello is a fan of show-the-flag management... Jeff Bercovici, "Twitter's CEO: How I Stay Focused Under Fire," *Inc. Magazine*, March 2015 (www.inc.com/magazine/201503/jeff-bercovici/how-dick-costolo-keeps-his-focus.html).

She sees common mistakes... Megan McArdle, "Obamacare Shouldn't Have Been Managed Like a Campaign," Bloomberg View, November 5, 2013 (www.bloombergview.com/articles/2013-11-05/obamacare-shouldn-t-have-been-managed-like-a-campaign).

Buy copies in bulk... George Anders, "Microsoft's Leadership Flip," *LinkedIn Pulse*, May 21, 2014 (https://www.linkedin.com/pulse/20140521194402-59549-microsoft-s-leadership-flip).

CHAPTER 11: Graceful Exits

An ongoing Gallup survey... Amy Adkins, "Majority of U.S. Employees Not Engaged Despite Gains in 2014," Gallup, Washington, DC (www.gallup.com/poll/181289/majority-employees-not-engaged-despite-gains-2014.aspx). See also *The State of Employee Engagement/Fall 2014*, Modern Survey, Minneapolis, MN (www.modernsurvey.com/wp-content/uploads/2014/11/The-State-of-Engagement-Report-Fall-2014.pdf).

A highly selective filtering process... Dr. John Sullivan, "Why You Can't Get a Job... Recruiting Explained by the Numbers," ERE Recruiting Intelligence, May 20, 2013 (www.eremedia.com/ere/why-you-cant-get-a-job-recruiting-explained-by-the-numbers).

Resume readers now spend an average of six seconds... Will Evans, "Keeping an Eye on Recruiter Behavior," The Ladders, 2012 (cdn.theladders.net/static/images/basicSite/pdfs/TheLadders-EyeTracking-StudyC2.pdf).

A non-trivial investment of time and money... "There Are Significant Business Costs to Replacing Employees," Center for American Progress, November 9, 2012 (www.scribd.com/doc/112707536/There-Are-Significant-Business-Costs-to-Replacing-Employees).

Using HR as talent spotters... Kyle Smith, "It's Time for Companies to Fire Their Human Resource Departments," Forbes.com, April 4, 2014 (onforb.es/10IDElt).

Laszlo Bock described the results of an internal analysis... Adam Bryant, "On GPAs and Brainteasers: New Insights from Google on Recruiting and Hiring," LinkedIn Pulse, June 20, 2013. See also Laszlo Bock, Work Rules! (2015).

Heidrik & Struggles revealed its own scorecard... Brooke Masters, "Rise of a Headhunter," Financial Times, March 30, 2009 (www.ft.com/cms/s/0/19975256-1af2-11de-8aa3-0000779fd2ac.html#axzz3oNoUkMUL).

A soup Nazi... A famous Seinfeld TV episode in 1995 introduced a militant restaurant manager who yelled "no soup for you!" at customers.

A classic movie... The Devil Wears Prada (2006) (www.imdb.com/title/tt0458352).

The passion hypothesis is simply bad advice... Cal Newport, So Good They Can't Ignore You (2012).

A long and very personal learning process... Chester Elton, "Take This Job and Love It," LinkedIn Pulse, August 16, 2014 (https://www.linkedin.com/pulse/20140816194303-39785422-take-this-job-and-love-it).

Dilbert cartoonist Scott Adams... Scott Adams, "Fail Your Way to Success," The Wall Street Journal, October 12-13, 2013 (www.wsj.com/articles/ SB10001424052702304626104579121813075903866).

Others would gladly work for free... Chandra Bozelko, "My Prison Job Wasn't About the Money," The Wall Street Journal, October 12, 2015 (www.wsj.com/articles/my-prison-job-wasnt-about-the-money-1444600577).

Famous for an I quit video message... Marina Shifrin, "Want to Quit Your Job? Make These Smart Money Moves," Glamour, April 29, 2014 (www.glamour.com/inspired/2014/04/how-to-save-money-and-quit-your-job-marina-shifrin-shares-her-tips).

It's helpful to remember... J.T. O'Donnell, "Employer Loved Me... Then Rejected Me," LinkedIn Pulse, January 29, 2015 (https://www.linkedin.com/pulse/employer-loved-me-rejected-j-t-o-donnell).

A personal style that's often in conflict... Susan Cain, "The Rise of the New Groupthink and the Power of Working Alone," LinkedIn Pulse, June 3, 2015 (https://www.linkedin.com/pulse/rise-new-groupthink-power-working-alone-susan-cain.

PART II: Personal Stories

"Silver Dolphins": Alex Munkachy is currently writing technical documentation for several FBI software systems. He also writes creative fiction, teaches English, and runs a popular comedy account on Twitter under the pen name Wanda LaQuanda.

"I was... interesting": Jonathan Rotenberg is an executive coach and management consultant. He is currently writing a memoir entitled *My Teacher Steve Jobs*.

"As invisible as wallpaper": Marielle Rabins has been a campus recruiter for the AmeriCorps City Year program in Atlanta. She is currently an undergraduate at Emory University.

"100% different from school": Richard Twiddy is an automotive technician at the Glenmore Audi Parts and Service center in Calgary, Alberta.

"A complete know-it-all": Therese Reger is an independent journalist and editor who has worked for The Wall Street Journal, built a successful medical newsletter business, and now contributes to several blogs.

"I have some notes to be typed": Carol McKeen recently retired after 25 years as an employee benefits consultant and vice president at Aon Consulting.

"Communicating with aliens": Wendy Clark is the lead singer with the Wendy Clark Band (formerly Tequila Mockingbird) and is a freelance Web designer and marketing consultant.

"I wrote my own job description": Mark Flanagan has been a senior executive with several major software companies, including Lotus, Kurzweil Applied Intelligence, and Envox. He is currently the CEO of Twin Peaks Research, a training startup for software developers.

"Two patients": Cynthia Ghazary is a Deaf Studies major at California State University/Northridge (CSUN).

"Christmas in July": Whitney Shepperson is a graduate of the Virginia Commonwealth University School of Business and now works as a lab and safety coordinator at Tredegar Films.

"Beard Employment": Kai Cofer has appeared in more than thirty Hollywood and TV film productions, usually playing characters with long beards.

"Bonded forever": Patricia Smith is a well-known painter, co-author of a cookbook, and performing artist.

"Surrounded by Eskimos": Sath Sathyanarayan is a management consultant who helps high-tech companies fine-tune their offshore and outsourced operations.

"Folding laundry": Jasmin Skinner is an orthodontic technician who is currently taking care of her new baby. "Yes, I'm still folding a lot of laundry," she says.

"My co-workers were less than thrilled": Kelly Moran is a guest services supervisor for the Calgary Flames.

"It wasn't the job I wanted": Luis Rodriguez currently works as a video editor for CNN.

PART III: The New-Job Playbook

Introduction... Ken Kuang, "Teaching Entrepreneurs to Do More Than Dream," *The Wall Street Journal*, August 18, 2015 (www.wsj.com/articles/teaching-entrepreneurs-to-do-more-than-dream-1439852625).

How to Leverage an Internship... Matt Meuleners, "What's My Name?" Focus Training (medium.com/@FOCUS_leaders/whats-my-name-7c20afaf46e1)

How to Deliver a Compelling Presentation... Carmine Gallo, "The Presentation Secrets of Steve Jobs," (www.presensatie.nl/wp-content/uploads/2014/08/Presentation-Secrets-Of-Steve-Jobs.pdf); Joe Queenan, "Speak No Evil," *The Wall Street Journal*, June 14-15, 2014; "Secrets of a Great TED Talk," *Inc. Magazine*, October 2013; Hugh Culver, "How to Deliver a Great Speech," (hughculver.com/how-to-deliver-a-great-speech); Leigh Buchanon, "Give the Audience More of What It Wants: Less," *Inc. Magazine,* October 2013; Dave Paradi, "Five Tips to Make PowerPoint Presentations More Effective," Think Outside the Slide (www.thinkoutsidetheslide.com/five-tips-to-make-PowerPoint-business-presentations-more-effective).

How to Run a Great Meeting... Sean Blanda, "How to Run Your Meetings Like Apple and Google," (99u.com/articles/7220/how-to-run-your-meetings-like-apple-and-google); Patrick Lencioni, *Death by Meeting* (2004); Camille Sweeney and Josh Gosfield, "11 Simple Tips for Having Great Meetings," *Fast Company,* June 17, 2013 (http://www.ceo.com/news_and_insights/11-simple-tips-for-having-great-meetings/).

How to Become a Better Negotiator... Chris Bucholz, "Six Negotiating Tactics That Actual Professionals Use," Cracked, May 20, 2014, (www.cracked.com/blog/6-negotiating-tactics-that-actual-professionals-use); James Altucher, "The Ten Worst Things You Can Do In A Negotiation" (http://www.jamesaltucher.com/2015/03/the-ten-worst-things-you-can-do-in-a-negotiation); Don Maher, "PICOS: What It Is, How to Deal With It," RedChasm, February 2, 2011 (redchasm.com/achieving-sales-goals/picos-what-it-is-how-to-deal-with-it/); Jim Camp, *Start With No* (2002).

How to Interview a Customer... Kristin Zhivago, *Roadmap to Revenue* (2011).

How to Manage a Project... Joel Spolsky, *Joel on Software* (2004); Frederick P. Brooks, Jr., *The Mythical Man Month* (1975); Atul Gawande, *The Checklist Manifesto* (2010).

How to Manage a Budget... Michael Gonnerman, financial advisor, Hanover, NH.

How to Analyze Survey Results... Dr. Frederick Van Bennekom, principal, Great Brook Consulting, Bolton, MA; Phil Verghis, CEO, Klever, Chapel Hill, NC.

How to Build a Business Forecast... Rick Kilton, principal, RWK Enterprises, Berthoud, CO; Burke Franklin, "Are Your Financial Projections Believable?" *LinkedIn Pulse*, June 29, 2015 (www.linkedin.com/pulse/your-financial-projections-believable-burke-franklin).

How to Manage Your Time... Amy Gallo, "Why Aren't You Delegating?" *Harvard Business Review*, July 26, 2012; Leigh Buchanan, "Inside the Psychology of Productivity," *Inc. Magazine*, March 2015 (www.inc.com/magazine/201503/leigh-buchanan/the-psychology-of-productivity.html).

Acknowledgments

To a large extent, this book rests on some 50 years of my own experience as a business writer and part-time management consultant, talking with people in a variety of industries about their problems and successes. I've learned a great deal from this experience (readers are free to disagree, of course), and I'm hugely grateful for this in-the-trenches view of the world.

Writing this book was also an excuse to explore the vast universe of books, articles, and research studies about business and career strategies. The collective expertise I found in print and online is literally awesome. (I should probably extend special thanks to Amazon for delivering fresh books to my front porch every few days. Jeff Bezos is my hero.)

I also owe special thanks to my friend Richard Rabins, a long-time software entrepreneur, who got excited about the "first hundred days" concept when we were chatting about possible book projects. "This is the one you should do," he said. So I did.

Ernest Hemingway once said, "The first draft of anything is shit." Fortunately, I was able to recruit a few family members and friends to read my own first draft and tell me what needed to be fixed. These first readers include Jane Farber, Jonathan Tarter, John Brodeur, Mike Gonnerman, Rick Kilton, Sam Klaidman, Sath Sathyanarayan, Ira Steinberg, and Fred Van Bennekom. Thanks, everyone. You made a difference.

Thanks also to the people who shared their own personal first-job stories: Alex Munkachy, Jonathan Rotenberg, Marielle Rabins, Richard Twiddy, Therese Reger, Carol McKeen, Wendy Clark, Mark Flanagan, Cynthia Ghazary, Whitney Shepperson, Kai Cofer, Patricia Smith, Sath Sathyanarayan, Jasmin Skinner, Kelly Moran, and Luis Rodriguez. You brought first-time job experiences to life in ways that I couldn't have done by myself.

And finally, to all the readers who have made my own career possible: You have a special place in my heart. Thank you.

—Jeffrey Tarter

Printed in Great Britain
by Amazon